"From the creative pen of Diana Davis and her daughter Autumn Wall comes the book *Across the Street and Around the World*. This book will assist your church or small group with new and exciting ways to become more involved in missions. Read the challenge these dear ladies share with God's people. Seek to implement the practical evangelism and missions suggestions to reach your community and the world. I am grateful for the ministry of Diana, her husband, and their family. We need people involved in missions and evangelism to reach every man, woman, boy, and girl with the gospel of Christ! Diana and Autumn provide effective and real-life ideas that can truly make a difference. God's blessing to you as you encourage others in reaching a new level of involvement in seeing the Great Commission come to pass."

—Dr. Frank S. Page, president and chief executive officer,
Southern Baptist Convention Executive Committee

"Have you ever wanted to get involved in a missions project but you just didn't know where to start? Diana Davis and her daughter Autumn Wall have taken the guesswork out of missions and provided hundreds of ideas to help an individual, church, or even a small group of friends get started. Be sure you read Chapter 1 first to discover the why of missions; it's not just about doing good deeds but a response to God's call to go. *Across the Street and Around the World* is filled with the most creative ideas for sharing Christ with our neighbors and communities here and all over the world."

—Wanda Lee, executive director,
National Woman's Missionary Union®

"This book will help 'every church leave the building' and go *Across the Street and Around the World* with the gospel. Our churches should be on mission with God and want to share the good news of Jesus. This book includes many practical tools on how to carry out that mission. I suggest you buy it and use the ideas to touch and change lives . . . *Across the Street and Around the World*."

—Dr. Craig E. Culbreth, lead catalyst of missions and ministries,
Florida Baptist Convention

"After reading this book, you will be out of excuses for not participating in God's mission to get the gospel to other people. There are more ideas here than can be done by any person or church. Read this book with spiritual sensitivity—looking for the projects and possibilities that leap off the page and demand to be done. Then, get going! No more excuses."

—Dr. Jeff Iorg, president,
Golden Gate Seminary

"You know what I love about this book? It's practical and brimming with one-step ideas to make a difference for Christ in a community. Filled with so many easy suggestions for ways to connect and share, Diana and Autumn have the pulse of today's Christian woman. I poured over ideas and more than once said, *Of course! Why didn't I think of that?* I would recommend this book to ministry leaders, wives and moms, and anyone who wants to make a difference in someone's life."

—Beth Harris, executive assistant to the pastor,
Olive Baptist Church

"Do you take the Great Commission seriously? Diana and Autumn have provided you a book filled with creative ideas for proclaiming the gospel. These are not gimmicks; they are good news methods for individuals and churches. Read and go tell!"

—Ted Traylor, pastor,
Olive Baptist Church

"Diana Davis and Autumn Wall have conspired together to produce a compelling handbook of strategies and tactics that are devastating to the spiritual darkness that has long suffocated our communities. For the sake of your neighbors, please read, dream, adapt, and courageously execute."

—Jeff Christopherson, vice president of Send Network,
North American Mission Board, and author of
Kingdom Matrix and *Kingdom First*

"I have had the privilege of knowing Autumn Wall for over 15 years. She and her husband, Yale, have not only lived out this message but have rallied, encouraged, and brought others into the reality of the power of reaching people with the love of Jesus who many times, would never be reached without them. Thank you, Autumn and Diana, for putting together this work. We are blessed by your life and look forward to the impact this book will have for the kingdom of God."

—Jimmy Seibert, senior pastor, Antioch Community Church, and president, Antioch Ministries International

"Diana Davis is unique among leaders—an everyday visionary casting an array of fresh ideas for God's people to make an eternal difference among empty, hurting souls. And now her fresh ideas in *Across the Street and Around the World*—remarkably written with her daughter Autumn Wall—are poised to stir the body of Christ in ways they might never have imagined apart from this visionary's passion for the church to convey the wondrous news of Jesus throughout our communities, across our nation and around the world."

—Art Toalston, senior editor, Baptist Press, and author of *When I Meditate*

Other New Hope books by Diana Davis

Six Simple Steps: Find Contentment and Joy as a Ministry Wife

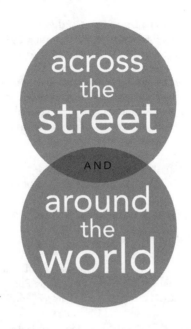

across the street AND around the world

IDEAS to SPARK MISSIONAL FOCUS

Diana Davis & Autumn Wall

NEW HOPE®
PUBLISHERS
Gospel-Centered. Missions-Driven.

Birmingham, Alabama

New Hope® Publishers
PO Box 12065
Birmingham, AL 35202-2065
NewHopePublishers.com
New Hope Publishers is a division of WMU®.

Library of Congress Cataloging-in-Publication Data

Names: Davis, Diana, 1952- author.
Title: Across the street and around the world : ideas to spark
missional focus / Diana Davis and Autumn Wall.
Description: Birmingham, AL : New Hope Publishers, 2016.
Identifiers: LCCN 2016013025 | ISBN 9781625915023 (sc)
Subjects: LCSH: Missions.
Classification: LCC BV2061.3 .D38 2016 | DDC 266--dc23
LC record available at http://lccn.loc.gov/2016013025

ISBN-13: 978-1-62591-502-3
N174101 • 0816 • 2.5M1

DEDICATION

Dedicated to our husbands, Steve Davis and Yale Wall, who live life on mission every day. It's a joy to be your partners in life, love, and mission.

‖‖‖‖‖‖‖‖‖‖‖‖‖

CONTENTS

HOW TO READ THIS BOOK
▮▮▮▮▮▮▮▮▮▮▮▮▮▮▮▮▮▮▮▮▮▮▮▮▮▮▮▮▮▮▮▮▮
17

INTRODUCTION
▮▮▮▮▮▮▮▮▮▮▮▮▮▮▮▮▮▮▮▮▮
19

chapter 1
ONE MANDATE
▮▮▮▮▮▮▮▮▮▮▮▮▮▮▮▮▮▮▮▮▮▮
21

chapter 2
ONE-HOUR MISSIONS IDEAS
||||||||||||||||||||||||||||||||||||||||||||||
31

chapter 3
ONE-DAY MISSIONS IDEAS
||||||||||||||||||||||||||||||||||||||||||||||
71

chapter 4

ONE-WEEK MISSIONS IDEAS

107

chapter 5

ONE LONG-TERM MISSIONS IDEA

135

chapter 6

ONE CHECKLIST FOR MISSIONS TRIPS

165

chapter 7

ONE BIG PLAN: GO!

187

CONCLUSION

199

APPENDIX

201

ACKNOWLEDGMENTS

A special thanks goes out to Nancy Schultze, Craig Culbreth, Laura Christopherson, Susan Matheus, Jim Witt, and to the editorial and marketing teams at New Hope Publishers for giving us great feedback throughout the writing of this book. Thanks to missionaries we have worked with around the world, church staff we've served alongside in local churches, and partners in ministry who have served on mission with us. You have been with us in the trenches as we have tried a million ideas on mission to reach people for Christ, and this book is a conglomeration of all of those efforts. Thanks also to Second Baptist Church in Springfield, Missouri, and Living Hope Church in Clarksville, Tennessee, for being incredible models of what it looks like for established churches to partner together with church planters to plant churches around the world together.

HOW TO READ THIS BOOK

The heartbeat of every Christian on earth has to be the mission of God. Are you intentionally living on mission with Him? In this book, you will find more than 1,000 practical missional ideas that you can cater to your situation, capabilities, and passions. But before we begin, we want to explain how to best utilize this book.

The only "required reading" in this book is Chapters 1 and 7. Really. Read Chapter 1 because it sets the pace for every idea in the book. Read Chapter 7 because it ties it all together. Everything in between is a resource. It's a book of ideas and projects, of lists and bullet points. Even so, we can have all the ideas in the world and launch the best events and projects anyone has ever seen, but if we don't start from a place of humility before God and brokenness for the lost around us, then it's only ideas. First, we go to God for the mandate of His plan for us, and then we set our feet to action in obedience of His will.

Next, settle into your coziest chair with a pen, a highlighter, and a cup of tea. Then, have at it! This book is a missions free-for-all, designed for you to enjoy and read interactively. Please jot notes obsessively.

Cross out ideas that won't work in your community. Circle ones that grab your attention. Write lots of notes when you have a better idea. Each time you turn another page, ask God again to show you what ways He wants to use your group or church to impact your world.

Through the pages of this book you will find 1,000 idea-generators that we've arranged in simple time segments:

1 Hour—quick missions projects you can accomplish in 60 minutes or less. Some take a little preparation; others just take a few minutes.

1 Day—longer projects to impact your community or world. You'll be amazed at what can be accomplished in less than 24 hours.

1 Week—out-of-town or out-of-country missions trips, plus other week-long missions projects you can do even in your own city.

Long-Term—ongoing or longer-term missions ideas, and quick thoughts about volunteer, part-time, and full-time missions service.

Each of these time segments is divided topically to help you navigate.

You'll also find an entire Chapter of tips to help you plan a team missions trip across town, across the continent, or across the world. It can be intimidating to think about taking a group from your church on an overseas trip or even across the country on mission. There are so many details to plan and decisions to make. This Chapter will help you know the right questions to ask and how to prepare your team as you go. We hope you'll highlight every line of this Chapter. Last, there's an urgent challenge to take action.

This book is written to inspire you and your small group or church to live on mission. Don't be overwhelmed. You know that God commands every Christian to live on mission for Him and that He also equips His followers with His power and will. Remember: "The one who calls you is faithful, and he will do it" (1 Thessalonians 5:24 NIV). Pray for His wisdom and prompting as you read.

So grab your pen, and get ready for brain drain. We're praying that you'll become so enthused you'll hardly be able to finish a page before starting a project.

But that's OK. This isn't a reading book. It's a *going* book.

INTRODUCTION

We are a unique pair of authors—a mother and daughter. Together we have been on so many missions trips and participated in so many missions projects that we've had a hard time even recounting all of them as we sat to write this book.

Diana previously authored four Christian books, and writes the syndicated column, "Fresh Ideas." She and her husband, Steve, served as pastor and wife in a church plant as well as small and large Texas churches. Diana gained an even broader picture of missions when Steve served as Indiana Baptists's state director and now serves as vice president of the North American Mission Board.

Autumn and her pastor/husband, Yale, are currently planting Living Faith Church in Indianapolis, Indiana, where she also serves as the worship leader. She has served in churches large and small in Texas and Indiana and also helped plant a church in Sheffield, England.

We've both had extensive experience and joy in doing missions in our communities and around the world. We've been strategically involved in exciting missions projects in our local churches. Combined, we've been involved in missions in 42 states and 13 countries. Most of these suggestions come from our personal experiences and observations. We've also included some fun stories of our missions experiences.

Most importantly, we both have a "real life," too. We work. We play. We enjoy family and friends and hobbies. We know that when we live life purposely on mission for Christ, He uses every aspect of our lives to spread His Light.

We hope this book inspires your church or small group and ignites you to intentionally live every minute of life on mission for God.

chapter 1

ONE MANDATE

Go and make disciples of all nations, baptizing them in the name of the Father and of the Son and of the Holy Spirit and teaching them to obey everything I have commanded you. And surely I am with you always, to the very end of the age. —Matthew 28:19–20 (NIV)

Sure, you've heard these words, the last words Jesus spoke before ascending into heaven. You probably even skimmed over it just now as you read because it's so familiar. But we have one question for you: *are you going?*

As Christians and as the church, it's easy to get caught up in our ministry to each other and simply lose sight of this command of our Savior to go. Don't get me wrong, ministry within the church is needed and important, but if we end our ministry within the walls of the church we are missing out on a huge part of the commands of God! We need to be on mission in our world.

Sure, we talk about going. We do Bible studies and sermon series about it. We sing about it. Or we read books on it. But when was the last time your church or small group went out and did something to bring the lost in your area to Christ? James 1:22 says, "Do not merely listen to the word, and so deceive yourselves. *Do what it says*" (NIV, authors' emphasis).

Here's the punch line of missions: it's not missions unless you're going!

WHY BE ON MISSION?
||||||||||||||||||||||||||||||||||

Think for a minute about your life. What have been your greatest moments of joy and excitement? What have been your deepest valleys of pain? What about major decisions you have made in your life? As you walk through life *knowing Jesus*, you probably make major decisions for your family *by praying with your spouse and seeking God's direction*. When pain and trials come, you probably spend hours crying *out to God for rescue, healing, deliverance, safety, comfort, and peace*. In great moments of life, you probably find yourself *worshiping and thanking God for His provision and blessing*. Now go back and read this paragraph, but insert the word **"alone"** for every phrase that is italicized.

That's how the vast majority of our world is living. Not just a life without religion. It's a life without hope. Without peace. Without someone to cry out to in times of pain and confusion or to rejoice with in good times. Without a community of people who unconditionally love, serve, and enjoy each other—called the church. Without purpose and direction. It's a life alone. The longer we live as believers the more difficult it can be to remember what life was like without Jesus, but as we begin to recall the emptiness we felt before Christ we are reminded of the urgency of this mission to go make disciples of all nations.

Matthew 24:14 says, "And this gospel of the kingdom will be preached in the whole world as a testimony to all nations, and then the end will come" (NIV). Let's get real. Statistically, we have a long way to go for the gospel to be preached in the whole world. The International Mission Board did a study that showed more than 2 billion people in the world today have no affiliation with Christ. David Platt, president of the International Mission Board, spoke at the Send North America Conference in 2015 challenging believers to be broken over this enormous number: 2 billion. We have to put feet to our message. They have identified 3,200 people groups in the world who have not been engaged with the gospel. That means not only have they not heard the gospel, but there is no one even trying right now to share with them.

They don't have a copy of the Bible in their language. They don't have a gospel-preaching church in their area.

Bring that statistic closer to home, and we see that the percentage of people living in the United States of America who have no relationship with Jesus is rapidly increasing every year. Often, the church does a great job caring for its own, but it seems we're lacking in the going. The harsh truth is, we are not reaching the rapidly growing population around us fast enough.

Something has to change. It isn't enough to be good people and hope that someone asks us, "What must I do to be saved?" We have to be vocal about our faith. We have to stand up for the truth and values in Scripture and lovingly lead people to Jesus.

So where does it start? We get it—it's hard to think about these numbers and statistics without being overwhelmed with our inadequacy to do anything to make a significant dent when we're battling our own life just trying to pay our bills, get kids to school on time, or pass a class.

When I was in college, I remember hearing friends speaking about reaching the lost. They challenged me to start by praying one simple prayer every day, "God, break my heart for the lost." That's the starting point. We have to begin the pursuit of missions with the pursuit of the heart of God. When my heart is broken—genuinely broken—for the people across the street and around the world who have no relationship with Jesus, then my mission changes from being self-focused to being committed to whatever it takes to see people come to Christ. Our friend Jeff Christopherson, vice president of the Send Network at the North American Mission Board, often asks the question, "What's worse than being lost? Being lost with no one looking for you."

God has placed you where you are to make an impact on the individuals you interact with every day and to lead them to Him. When we pray daily for God to break our hearts for the lost, He begins to show us who is lost around us and then we begin to put feet to the gospel. Remember the armor of God in Ephesians 6? It's fitting that the shoes are fitted with the readiness of the gospel of peace (v. 15). It takes feet, action, and movement to see the gospel spread.

BE ON A MISSION FOR CHRIST
||||||||||||||||||||||||||||||||||||||||||||||

So what actually is missions?

→ A group or committee of persons sent to a foreign country to conduct negotiations, establish relations, provide scientific and technical assistance, or the like.

→ The business with which such a group is charged.

→ Any important task or duty that is assigned, allotted, or self-imposed.

→ An important goal or purpose that is accompanied by strong conviction; a calling or vocation.

→ A sending or being sent for some duty or purpose.

→ Those sent.

Each of these definitions points to a focused task, but for the purpose of this book, we add the phrase, "Christian missions must be done in Jesus' name and for the ultimate purpose of sharing Him with those who don't know Him."

This may seem like a no-brainer—of course we want to be on mission for Christ. That's why we're picking up this book! But it stands as a good reminder that nothing about missions has anything to do with us other than our simple obedience to say "yes."

Our world is full of people who are striving to do good deeds. Universities require students to complete community service hours. Corporations are looking to donate chunks of cash to charities. People like those who "give back." My neighbor just returned from a "missions trip" that had no connection with God. It was just well-intentioned people doing well-intentioned things.

But we, as Christians, need to remember that Jesus called us to do these things in His name, not in our own. If the purpose of your good deed, missions project, or missions trip is to let others know how good you are, it's not missions. Every mission must be in Jesus' name, and for the purpose of sharing Him with those who don't know Him.

Missions is much bigger than your reputation. It's more purposeful than a good project or trip. Our missional acts of kindness must be done in His name, or they're just random acts of kindness.

So you give food to the hungry in Jesus' name. You take a missions trip to Amsterdam or New York so you can point people to God. You go to the gym with the intention of sharing Jesus with someone while you lift weights. You help plant a church so more people can know Him. You do good things in the community for the single purpose of glorifying and sharing Him. Instead of observing what a great person you are, people notice what a great God you serve.

||||||||||||||

Our church took a college missions trip to St. Louis one spring break. One of the students who went on the trip with us had been on multiple missions trips before: building homes, serving in orphanages, etc. with other churches and signed up to join us. It wasn't until we were on the trip and sharing the gospel with people that she realized she didn't have a relationship with God and gave her life to Jesus! All of the years spent in church—even going on missions trips—and she had never understood the gospel. Don't let your missions trip be just about doing good deeds. It has to be about Jesus.

||||||||||||||

Second Corinthians 5:20 says, "Therefore, we are ambassadors for Christ, certain that God is appealing through us. We plead on Christ's behalf, 'Be reconciled to God'" (HCSB). As we go out on mission we must continually keep Christ as our goal. He is the goal of our hearts as we seek to bring joy to His heart through what we do and how we do it with excellence. He is the goal of the mission—for all people to know Him and call Him Lord. He is the goal for each individual we encounter on mission as we purpose to draw them one step closer to knowing Him.

Paul prayed,

That the Messiah may dwell in your hearts through faith. I pray that you, being rooted and firmly established in love, may be able to comprehend with all the saints what is the length and width, height and depth of God's love, and to know the Messiah's love that surpasses knowledge, so you may be filled with all the fullness of God. —Ephesians 3:17–19 (HCSB)

BE ON A MISSION TOGETHER
IIIIIIIIIIIIIIIIIIIIIIIIIIIIIIIIIIIIIIIIIIIIIII

Your church or small group was designed by the hand of God to be a launching pad for missions in your community and around the world. There are many good things you can do on your own to reach out to people, engage the lost, and serve your community, but when you do it together for the glory of God it only intensifies the power in the movement. There are so many Scriptures about being better together.

As iron sharpens iron, so a friend sharpens a friend. —Proverbs 27:17

A person standing alone can be attacked and defeated, but two can stand back-to-back and conquer. Three are even better, for a triple-braided cord is not easily broken. —Ecclesiastes 4:12

Now these are the gifts Christ gave to the church: the apostles, the prophets, the evangelists, and the pastors and teachers. Their responsibility is to equip God's people to do his work and build up the church, the body of Christ. This will continue until we all come to such unity in our faith and knowledge of God's Son that we will be mature in the Lord, measuring up to the full and complete standard of Christ. —Ephesians 4:11–13

How wonderful and pleasant it is when brothers live together in harmony! —Psalm 133:1

At the same time, God's hand was on the people in the land of Judah, giving them all one heart to obey the orders of the king and his officials, who were following the word of the LORD. —2 Chronicles 30:12

Just as our bodies have many parts and each part has a special function, so it is with Christ's body. We are many parts of one body, and we all belong to each other. —Romans 12:4

The human body has many parts, but the many parts make up one whole body. So it is with the body of Christ. Some of us are Jews, some are Gentiles, some are slaves, and some are free. But we have all been baptized into one body by one Spirit, and we all share the same Spirit. —1 Corinthians 12:12–13

When God created this earth and the perfect Garden of Eden, the only thing He said was "not good" was "for the man to be alone" (Genesis 2:18 HCSB). From day one, God created us to need each other. Every mission He speaks to your heart is, by definition, intended to be for you and someone else. Even when you look at the New Testament picture of Paul spreading the church around the world, we always see a team go together. Paul and Barnabas, Paul and John Mark, Paul and Timothy, Paul and Titus, Paul and Silas, Paul and Luke . . . even the great missionary-church planter Paul didn't try to do it alone! And neither should we.

This book of missions ideas is written with partnership in mind. Some of the ideas could be done alone, but we hope you'll consider doing missions as a church or a small group. If you are a massive church with tons of resources or a brand new church plant with no building, you can take these ideas and format them to your ministry. You'll be energized and encouraged by one another and you'll gain a fresh perspective of the heart of God as you begin to be on mission together.

BE ON A MISSION THAT IS RADICAL
||||||||||||||||||||||||||||||||||||||||||||||||||||

As the church, if we want to make an impact on those 2 billion people, worldwide, or on the people in our backyard without relationship with Christ (a number that grows with each passing year), it's going to take radical faith, radical decisions, and radical obedience. We can no longer expect the world to come to the church for answers, hope, or peace. We must be intentional and radical in our actions to find the way to go to them.

This means stepping outside of our comfort zone. It means going to places where we probably wouldn't normally venture. It means saying, "Here I am, send me," instead of, "Here I am, fill me." It means being willing to release our children as ambassadors for Christ wherever He calls them. It means considering the option of uprooting our family from a comfortable lifestyle into a radical lifestyle of obedience that is willing to go anywhere and do anything to reach the lost and see churches planted and strengthened all over our nation and the nations of the earth. These things don't come naturally. They take people willing to sacrifice what they want, to instead be on mission for what God wants.

If you are waiting for the right time or right circumstances before you step out in a radically obedient faith-filled venture of life that God is calling you to, you'll probably never go. When God spoke to Moses from the burning bush, Moses expressed his inadequacy. God reminded Moses that He would be with him. When Daniel was brought into captivity in Babylon, he was in a foreign culture with foreign gods and expectations contrary to his beliefs. He was just a teen, but God used those uncomfortable moments to launch a life of influence. When God called Jeremiah, he objected that he was too young, but God said, "I have put my words in your mouth!" So what's the key to stepping out on faith into radical obedience? It's nothing less than a life surrendered to the fullness of the Holy Spirit. That's what launched Simon Peter on the day of Pentecost to preach, and 3,000 were saved. Radical obedience! The truth is, you'll never feel ready. That's why it's called radical obedience!

Often we like to do things that are comfortable. We go on a trip to a place we've been before so there are not as many surprises. We include only a small group of people because we made a great team together last time. But the reality is, when we stay comfortable in our mission, what we are really seeking is control over the situation. The more comfortable we are, the less we have to trust God to move. Instead of staying comfortable and content, be bold this year and step out into the deep water like Peter did when he stepped out of the boat and walked on water with Jesus (Matthew 14). When we give up control over the situation and step out in faith that God can do something absolutely impossible, we will be amazed at the ways He shows up in His strong power! And that's a story to come home with at the end of the trip.

SO, WILL YOU?

Will you take seriously God's mandate to go? These next Chapters contain a hefty collection of fresh, simple ideas for a church or small group to reach outside the church walls and impact the lost. We're praying that God will use some of them to inspire you to joyful action to engage people outside of your church, with the end goal of sharing the story of Jesus.

Remember: praying and giving is necessary for the church. But praying and giving without going is like dishing up a huge bowl of the best ice cream, putting all your favorite toppings on, then leaving it on the counter to melt and throw away. Without the element of going and doing, we miss the point of missions. Jesus said, "Go and make disciples of all the nations" (Matthew 28:19), not, "stay and pray for disciples to be made in all the nations." So how are you praying, how are you giving, and, most importantly, how are you going?

Life is busy and chaotic, and everything around you is vying for your attention. We get it. But what if God infused missions in the midst of your everyday chaos? What if He gave you purpose for every mundane moment and clear direction in every nail biting decision? Well, He has: go and make disciples of all nations. And you know what it means to "go"? It's not tricky—it means to "not stay." So read on in this book and get some ideas that will excite you and your church or small group to go and be a part of God's great mission to make disciples together.

chapter 2

ONE-HOUR MISSIONS IDEAS

e know life can be busy. As a spouse and parent, you work long hours to provide for your family and race to ball games and school concerts so your kids know you support them. As a single adult, you balance your job, hobbies, and friendships. As a business-person who travels a lot, you don't want to miss out on time with your family. As a college student, you cram for tests, read more than you have ever read in your life, and try not to blow up at your roommate for leaving dishes undone *again*. As a homemaker, you try to get laundry done, dinner ready, the house clean for your mother-in-law's visit, and everyone out the door with both shoes on today. The list goes on and on. You have a busy sched-ule but still want to make an impact on your world, how does that all fit together?

You may not have eight hours a day to do missions projects . . . but try a one-hour missions project to start your journey into missional living this week! As a family, a small group, or a whole church, these ideas are designed with your busy schedule in mind. You'll be shocked at how much can be accomplished in 60 minutes or less. Make the most of the time you have by being intentional in sharing the love of Jesus.

Are you the leader of a small group? Pick an idea from this sec-tion as a project your small group can do during your weekly meet-ing. As your group arrives and settles in for Bible study, take time to pray together, then pull out the supplies for a one-hour idea and serve together. It will be a night they won't quickly forget.

A church might plan a quarterly one-hour project on a Saturday or Sunday afternoon. A women's group could add an hour to their regular meeting and divide into ministry teams to accomplish their missions outside the church building. Youth, singles, and senior adults will find plenty of great ideas they'll enjoy. There's nothing that brings unity to a Christian group more than being on mission for God together.

Remember to include a homemade card with a note about God's love, a printed invitation to your church, or a personal word of witness. These aren't just good deeds; these are good deeds done in Jesus' name, with the intention of sharing Him with the lost.

These idea-starters can inspire you to get missional. Sixty minutes really can make a difference in eternity. Ready? Go!

FOR THE CHURCH NEIGHBORHOOD

It's possible for a church or small group to be very aware of lost people in the nations of the world but to ignore those who live a block from the church. Begin missions in your own Jerusalem—the neighborhood surrounding your church. Each time you drive or walk to church, see the people who live nearby. Pray for them. And make a plan to share Jesus with them. Try one of these ideas:

Talking Sidewalks. Do pedestrians regularly use your church sidewalk? Recruit a team of artistic church members to create chalk art that may include encouraging Scripture or invitations to church events.

Share Your View. Does your church lawn provide an awesome view of your town's fireworks show or parade?

➜ Use social media and outdoor banners to invite folks in town to bring a chair and watch the event from your church lawn.

➡ Members take a servant role, helping families, serving lemon-ade, making friends, and inviting everyone to Sunday worship.

➡ Be gracious with your resources and facilities.

➡ Consider including a cookout or barbecue to feed your guests.

➡ Offer a five-minute tour of your church building (classroom area, auditorium, etc., pointing out ministry and missions).

➡ Have a team of people come early to pray together over your church property as you prepare to bring in the community. Prayer walk the whole area and ask God to soften the ground so people can know Him here today.

A Flowery Invitation. Everyone loves flowers in springtime. Designate a Sunday where you encourage church members to bring a flowering potted plant to church. After the worship service that day, send the church out to the homes surrounding your church building and deliver a potted plant to every home on your block along with an invitation to church next Sunday.

Lawn Chair Concert. Post outdoor signs that read, "Free concert and ice cream on the lawn Friday at 6 o'clock. Bring your lawn chair or blan-ket!" Prepare an outdoor stage and a quality lineup of live Christian music. Add tiki torches or stringed lights, outdoor fans, and sidewalk chalk for kids. Church members serve watermelon or homemade ice cream, intentionally reaching out to guests.

Snow Crowd. On a good snow day, members and attenders meet to build dozens of snowmen on the church lawn. If neighbors stop by, encourage them to help. Decorate snow-families with creative props, and make signs on sticks, such as, "Life with Jesus is snow much fun," "There's snow way I'm missing church this week," or, "See you here Sunday!" to invite folks to church. Send a quality digital photo to the local paper. It might make the front page.

Move Outside. Take church outside during summer months to create missional purpose to your worship service. Simply set up chairs and a sound system outside and do your normal worship service on your church lawn. Put up large banners and yard signs that say, "Come worship with us," then be on the lookout for guests.

Snow Shoveling Party. During extended extreme weather, shovel home sidewalks for church neighbors or the elderly in the church vicinity. When neighbors ask, "Why?" tell them about Jesus' love for them.

Drive-By Witness. Does your church have an interchangeable outdoor sign? Make the message evangelistic! Advertise events that the unchurched community might want to attend at your church. Make your sign something that people want to drive by.

||||||||||||||

One church in our city always has a great sign. My husband and I enjoy it so much we intentionally drive out of our way to go past the church on our way home from work just to read what they have on it that week because we know it will make us smile to see what God is doing through their ministry. They're known in town as the church with the great sign. Gotta be known for something!

||||||||||||||

Rolls of Quarters. Have members of a small group collect quarters and go together to a local laundry for an hour. As they hang out together, when someone comes in to do laundry, they pay for their machines.

➡ As they casually visit with the people, God opens opportunities to share about Him.
➡ The group could also bring nice laundry detergent or pods and dryer sheets to share.
➡ Take opportunities to share about Jesus.
➡ Even better, if there is room in your church, purchase a washer

and dryer, and allow folks who don't have their own machines to use them. This could be an outdoor closet area or a section of your fellowship hall.

Walk-In Movie. Project a family movie on an outdoor wall, provide free popcorn and drinks, and invite the whole town. Members bring extra blankets and lawn chairs to share.

GET → GOING!

Look at the homes near your church. Ask God to show you ways to share Him with those who live within a "stone's throw" of your church.

Come to Our Playground. Does your church have an indoor playground? Share it, especially during summer or winter months when extreme heat or cold keep children from playing outside. Open it up to anyone in the community to register their kids for one-hour slots to come play. Have church members assigned to each hour to visit with parents as kids play.

Giggles and Sprinkles Party. Plan an awesome event on the church playground or lawn for parents and preschoolers. Moms invite other preschool moms, and all guests receive an invitation to church. The party can include:

→ Water sprinklers
→ A bubble machine
→ Water balloon piñatas with waterproof prizes inside
→ An impromptu kazoo band
→ If it's a hot day, freeze a bunch of small toys in a large bowl of water. Dump out the ice block, and let the kids use their hands to free the toys from their prison of ice.
→ Moms in your church can initiate conversations with guests about parenting with the heart of Jesus.

FOR CHURCH OUTREACH EVENTS
||||||||||||||||||||||||||||||||||||||||||||||||||

God has blessed your church with many resources. How will you use them to be on mission for Him? Take a fresh look at ministries and events you already do at your church or small group. How can you add an outreach focus? Could a small change make it missional? Try one of these one-hour ideas:

We Care About Day Care Families. If your church has a day care program, invite those parents to church. They may be waiting for an invitation! Mail a letter from the pastor and day care director each fall. Encourage teachers and parents who are church members to invite day care families to a small group and worship service. Send home a current list of upcoming family activities and opportunities at the church.

Men's and Women's Events. Ladies' luncheons or men's breakfasts can be a very effective missions project when you refocus your event with unchurched friends in mind. One favorite plan is to have a speaker who shares personal stories of God's impact and presents the gospel. A decision may be indicated with an X on their door prize card, and follow up contact is made the same day.

|||||||||||||||

As I chatted with a first-time guest at church, she gleamed, "Three different ladies invited me to be their guest at Thursday's luncheon!" Our quarterly ladies' luncheons were an awesome outreach arm of the church. They were beautifully decorated. The program was fun, fast-paced, evangelistic, and inspirational. They always ended precisely on time, so many working women brought work associates. And church members intentionally brought unchurched guests.

|||||||||||||||

Bring-Your-Sports-Team-to-Church Sunday. Do your kids play soccer? Does your husband play softball? Does your wife do roller derby? Pick a Sunday and get your whole team to come to church together that day. Meet ahead of time to carpool together. Plan a picnic and a game after church and let your team take on the church staff or your small group in their sport.

Friend Day. It's amazing how well Friend Day works at many churches. Encourage everyone to bring an unchurched friend, plan a special lunch or kids events, and get to know all those friends.

New Kids Welcome. Invite the community to attend your kids' camps, Vacation Bible School, or Wednesday night suppers. You may be surprised how many participate when invited.

GET→GOING! *Look hard at the programs and ministries inside your church. Ask God to reveal new ways you can improve them to reach others for Him.*

Honor Veterans on Veteran's Day. Advertise to invite every veteran in the community to come to worship on the Sunday before Veteran's Day. Plan a simple after-church reception in their honor. Express appreciation and present a gift bag with a military Bible, a tract, and a handwritten appreciation note from a teen in your church. Personally invite each guest to come again next week.

Christmas Craft Party. Organize a community-wide family Christmas craft party and help families make an artistic keepsake nativity scene as the leader shares the real Christmas story.

Christmas Eve Service. Make this the best event of the year: a brief, family-friendly Christmas Eve candlelight service. Plan far ahead for quality greeters and music. Invite the entire community, and be friendly when they arrive.

Christmas Day Service. Plan a short celebration on Christmas morning around 10 a.m. for families to come celebrate Jesus together. Bring your whole extended family to sing Christmas carols and hear the real reason for Christmas.

FOR THE LOCAL SCHOOL
||||||||||||||||||||||||||||||||||||||

The church must care for its community, and especially for the children. Even if a nearby school is low-functioning and troubled—especially if that is true!—we must see that as a vast missions field. One church or small group can make an enormous difference. These simple one-hour projects can help. Try one of these ideas.

Embrace Football. Place an ad in the program for the local high school football games, theater productions, or choir concerts inviting students and their families to your church. Gear the ad toward unchurched readers. Ask a graphic artist in your church to design the ad. Invite the team and coaches to sit together in worship service one Sunday. Pray for them. Serve them a delicious steak dinner with all the trimmings. Find ways to show support for local schools.

We Love Teachers. A small group or entire church could orchestrate a huge signup to create big, beautiful snack baskets for the teachers' lounges at local schools. Individuals, classes, committees, and groups can all sign up, make the baskets, and deliver them to the schools the first week teachers return for school. Print a nice card of encouragement and prayers from the church. Deliver the gorgeous basket on the teachers' first workday before school begins.

Principal Assistance. Prepare jam-packed backpacks for elementary, middle, or high school students. Include needed, quality items such as school supplies, healthy snacks, a toy, gloves, and so on. Write a note from your church or small group to let the child know God cares, then give the backpacks to the local principal, nurse, or counselor to distribute as they see need. If you are willing to continue this ministry, leave your contact information and ask the principal to call when more backpacks are needed.

More Backpack Uses. Use the same idea above, but provide the backpacks to a local children's home, single mother's shelter, or similar ministry.

Hot Dog! Your small group or church could offer to staff the concessions stand at one high school ball game each year. Wear your church T-shirts and have fun as you serve people. Don't accept payment; just view it as an opportunity to serve the community.

▮▮▮▮▮▮▮▮▮▮▮▮▮▮

One year our church put together large, beautiful gift baskets for teachers at every school in our surrounding area. They were filled with goodies, gifts, and gift cards for the teachers as well as notes from children in our church saying, "Thank you for teaching at my school." At the end of the first week of school, we delivered the baskets to the teacher break rooms with a sign encouraging them and inviting them to church. That year, we had 25 teachers from our school district join our church.

▮▮▮▮▮▮▮▮▮▮▮▮▮▮

Custom Covers. Design graphic paper book covers for youth, featuring your church and youth group name, events, and Scriptures to encourage students.

We Want to Help. Send a note or make a call to the local school principal or nurse offering your small group to meet practical needs of students in their school. Then be ready to act quickly. Are there children who need a coat? School supplies? Shoes or socks? Let them know your church is willing and ready to meet those needs. Ask permission to put a note in the pocket or the bag saying, "Jesus loves you," or at least a card from the church.

Invite Me! If you're a youth minister or youth small group leader, join a student for school lunch every time you're invited. Encourage, disciple, meet friends, and buy dessert.

School Teacher Appreciation Sunday. On the first Sunday after school begins, plan a teacher appreciation event.

➡ Provide students with printed invitation cards they can present to their teacher (and principals, librarians, bus drivers, nurses, food servers, coaches, music teachers, homeschool teachers, professors, counselors, and other school personnel) the first week of school inviting them to come to the event.

➡ Have kids meet their guests and sit with them. Provide name tags for the teachers and, if possible, a small gift.

➡ During the worship service, have a special time of prayer for teachers. Invite all teachers in the room to stand where they are or to come down front. Present them a small gift, then ask all students in the room to gather around the teachers and pray for them as they start a new school year. Lead a prayer of commitment and commissioning, asking God's guidance for these leaders as they touch the lives of children this year.

➡ Commit as a church to pray regularly for them, and ask God to give them opportunities to show and share His love with students.

| | | | | | | | | | | | | | | |

When our church did a School Teacher Appreciation Day, we were shocked at the response. Students of every age were crowded at the doors, eagerly awaiting their teachers' arrival. At the after-worship outdoor fellowship in their honor, we served small cartons of chocolate milk with cookies, church members and students mingled and thanked teachers.

| | | | | | | | | | | | | | | |

Pray for Schools. Gather in local school parking lots for prayer one day before the school semester begins. Pray for teachers, students, and staff; ask God to provide ministry opportunities in the school. Afterward, prayer groups can caravan to the local ice cream shop for fellowship.

Back-to-School Party. Host a fast, fabulous party on the day before the school semester begins or right after the bell rings on the first day of school. Plan separately for middle schoolers, high schoolers, or elementary children. Encourage kids to bring and warmly include guests. Leaders of your church's youth and children's ministries can send kids home with a calendar of upcoming events, including Bible classes, choir, sports, family events, after-school ministries, and worship.

GET → GOING!

Stop and consider the school district in your community. How can your church or small group best impact that missions field for God?

First Day of School Parents' Breakfast. Host a coffee shop at the church or on the church lawn. Parents can gather for coffee, donuts, and prayer after they drop their children off for the first day of school. Invite the community and seat parents by their child's school and grade level for fellowship. Pray for the kids by name. Provide a list of youth and kids' activities and worship times at your church.

Volunteer as Mentors. Many schools solicit mentors for students who need extra help with reading or for other troubled students. Send your women's ministry team or small groups once a week for an hour. Then meet with the same student weekly.

Citywide End-of-School Party. Advertise in the local paper and through social media.

→ The planning team involves students, youth, Sunday School leaders, and parents, and the primary goal is to bring friends who don't currently attend church. The party doesn't have to be long, but it must be well-planned and lots of fun.

→ Use a creative theme, such as: sand volleyball bash for high school, pizza treasure hunt for middle school, or splash party for elementary.

→ Have plenty of food.

→ Play upbeat Christian music.

→ Distribute a summer church calendar.

→ Prioritize your guests and encourage your church's kids to invite others to be a part of their class or small group over the summer.

→ Well before the party, ask church members if they need summer employees. Print a list or make a job wall for party attenders. Challenge members to hire teens, including guests, who come to the party, and use the summer to share Jesus with them as they work.

FOR THE COMMUNITY

Your community needs to see your church outside the church walls, living for Jesus. There's nothing that can ignite church growth and maturity like purposeful missions action. Try one of these one-hour missions adventures and shine for Him in your own community.

Handbag with a Heart. Clean out your closet and pick out a purse (or two!) that you no longer use but is still in good condition. After cleaning it, fill it with useful items, such as a hairbrush, lipstick, and other women's items, and include a handwritten note about God's love. Put the stuffed purse in the trunk of your car, and when God prompts, give it to a needy person you see.

Job Search Training. Advertise in the community and offer a monthly class to help those who are unemployed. Address topics such as job readiness, goal setting, skills necessary to be a dependable employee, and application assistance. Assist with contacts. As an additional help, consider assisting with clothing for an interview. A "practice" interview might be helpful for some. Befriend the class attenders, and pray for them.

Mega-Tip Blessings. Challenge each small group in your church to eat out together at a restaurant one day this week. Each person contributes an extravagantly large tip in a group envelope. They can ask the server how they can pray for him or her, and personally pray if it seems appropriate. Present the generous tip while explaining God's love and giving an invitation to your church.

Sweating and Sharing. If your church has a gym or exercise room, share it with the community. Invite teens after school. Invite firefighters or the police department to take advantage of your gym. Welcome and include guests with God's love. As an individual or as a small group, commit to regular, hour-long workouts with the intention of sharing Jesus. Just lift weights, stair-step, or walk on the treadmill or track. Get to know guests who are exercising and seize opportunities to invite them to church or talk about God.

Show Up En Masse. Order colorful church T-shirts for your youth group or senior adult group to wear to a little league or high school ball game or other community event. Have fun, and watch for opportunities to invite people to church.

Peanut Butter with a Message. Collect peanut butter for your local food bank or church pantry. Take a little extra time to write, "God loves you!" in permanent marker on the top of each jar before donating.

Outdoor Baptism. Celebrate baptism outdoors in a local pond, river, or beach when the weather allows. As outsiders observe the excitement, include them and explain.

Apron Time. Serve food at the local homeless shelter. Pray while you serve. Sit and have conversations on your break.

|||||||||||||||

One of our college students and a group of her friends make sandwiches every week and take them to people who live under a bridge downtown. They sit and talk, eat lunch, and share about what Jesus is doing in their life each week. Discipleship at its finest!

|||||||||||||||

Monday Missions Projects. During summer break, plan a weekly hands-on missional event for fifth and sixth graders, or for high school, middle school, or even senior adults. Break for Vacation Bible School, of course, but that will probably only leave about eight Mondays during school summer break. Do it well, whether you have three or 50 participants each week. Begin at 10:30 a.m. with a one-hour action-packed missions project, then return to church for bagged lunches. Find one-hour projects in this book, or ask your pastor for ideas. Arrange transportation. Make it fun and exciting, with a focus on touching unchurched people with God's love. Organize one or more groups to prepare and serve bag lunches with special treats and listen as kids chat about their missions adventure. Lunch could be done by a senior adult group, women's ministry, missions team, or others.

Social Agencies. What type of social agencies works in your community? Meet with various agencies to inquire how your church might partner with them. Make a plan with your church's missions committee to meet those needs in Jesus' name. For example, your church could partner with a program for early prison release, providing special holiday meals and seasonal projects.

Pay It Backward. During one specific week, ask church members to drive through a fast food restaurant. As they pay their bill, also have them pay the bill for the car behind them. Leave a church business card or a, "God bless you," note for the recipient, and pray that God will be honored through those gifts.

Nail Salon. Get permission from a local nursing home events coordinator to have a nail salon day. Gather a group of ladies and teenage girls from your church and take an hour to paint the fingernails of all the ladies who live in the home. As you paint their nails, listen to their stories, pray for (and with) them, and be sure to share the gospel along the way.

|||||||||||||||||

Deacon Tom and his wife go to the nursing home every Tuesday and paint ladies' fingernails. Our women's ministry sends a team to several nursing homes once a month. Our girls' missions group bought Christmas decals for ladies' nails for their Christmas project. The ministries of touch and a listening ear are enormous opportunities to talk about Jesus.

|||||||||||||||||

Drama in the Park. Have your church drama team prepare outdoor vignettes to present in appropriate park or street settings as a witness. This could become a pop-up witness around town.

➡ Keep the skits rather short. They should be lively and done with excellence.
➡ Stage people in the audience who will converse with attendees and invite them to church.

→ Go bigger by adding an instrumental, vocal, or praise dance group.

→ Have someone share their testimony and the gospel before or after the drama.

→ Be sure to have follow-up cards so you can get contact information from people you connect with during the outreach. You'll want to call them later to invite them to church again.

On the Wall. Take a flyer about your church's next event into local coffee shops and restaurants. Ask if you can post the flyer on their community board. Give it to the manager to put in the employee lounge.

Juvenile Justice. Work with local county or state juvenile detention and treatment facilities in your area to establish a partnership. You might volunteer as mentors, prayer partners, tutors, coaches, or Bible teachers.

Park Ministry. Do you have a cool city park nearby? Take sidewalk chalk, bubbles, and jump ropes for all the kids. Share balloons, with an invitation to a church kids' event tied to them.

Quick Disaster Relief. When a disaster such as flooding occurs in your community, quickly ask all your group members to purchase $25 or $50 gift cards to the local grocery store. Walk the affected neighborhood wearing church T-shirts, give a card to each family, and pray with them.

Homeless Lunch Bag. Prepare a paper bag of nonperishable food. Involve your children in this project by letting them color the paper bag, write "Jesus loves you," and a favorite Scripture. When you see someone by the road that is hungry, give him or her the bag.

Homeless Bags. Keep resealable sandwich bags in your car, with an assortment of items that a needy person would enjoy, along with a small New Testament and a note from the church. Some examples: gloves, knit cap, list of community/religious resources, soap, washcloth, travel-size shampoo, socks, bottled water or juice boxes, wet wipes, lotion, cough drops, packaged food (jerky, cheese and crackers, self-open canned meat, power bar), a Scripture card, or witnessing tract. Include a church brochure or invitation card if your church is nearby. Consider adding a $10 gift card to a nearby fast food restaurant.

Homeless Bags for All. If your small group has the resources, collect and prepare as many bags as possible, and give them to church members to gift as they encounter people in need. Or they could deliver bags to an area of town where homeless gather at night.

▌▌▌▌▌▌▌▌▌▌▌▌▌▌

Our church's weekly women's ministry revamped to add a choice of one-hour mission teams after classes, going in twos or threes outside our church to minister in the community. We were amazed at what could be accomplished in one well-planned hour and ladies loved it. Our average weekly attendance soared from a dozen to more than 100 women! Going is a joy.

▌▌▌▌▌▌▌▌▌▌▌▌▌▌

Stuffed Animal Collection. Ask church members to donate new stuffed animals of all shapes and sizes. Tie a bow around their neck with a note that says, "Jesus loves you," and deliver to the local children's hospital, group children's homes, or fire station.

Bibs and Bibles. Plan a baby shower for a local pregnancy center. Include copies of Christian parenting books, and baby-friendly cardboard Bibles or children's Bible storybooks to be given to each new baby.

IIIIIIIIIIIIIII

A sewing group in our church made stuffed lambs. A craft group created handmade dolls. The ceramics class painted little personalized baby shoe ornaments. We prepared personalized New Testaments. Use the gifts of church members to create personal baby celebration gifts as a ministry.

IIIIIIIIIIIIIII

Group Home Game Night. If there's a children's group home in your area, take a stack of board games and a few families from your church and go play! Look each child in the eye and listen to their stories. Be an encouragement to them and pray for them as you play. It's crucial to take adults to this type of outreach. Grandmothers and grandfathers are wonderful. These children need mother and father, grandmother and grandfather figures interacting with them.

Prayerwalking Upgrade. Take prayer to the streets. An hour of prayer can make an eternal difference. As you pray, notice opportunities for your church or small group to minister to the community. Be sure to stop and talk with people along your route and share Jesus with them.

→ Do singles in your church bike? How about a prayer-biking plan?
→ If teens in your church are skaters, challenge them to prayer skate.
→ Would moms in your church enjoy stroller prayerwalking?
→ Invite members who fly often to pray for your city as they leave or arrive by plane.
→ Do you take the bus to work or school? Ride and pray.
→ Northerners could cross-country ski and pray.
→ Coastal Christians could prayer-swim.
→ How about a prayer-glide or prayer-ballooning, praying for your city as you view them from above? Get crazy. Pray everywhere.

Prayerwalking Assignment. Challenge each person in your church or small group to select their own targeted prayerwalking path. For example, if they prayerwalk one block around their residence, they could knock on each door to ask how they can pray. Then they check back monthly for updates and more prayer requests.

Correspond with an Inmate. If your church has a prison Bible correspondence ministry, you can grade a few studies and write those inmates in less than an hour. Be sure to correspond through the chaplain or a ministry program, without using your personal contact information.

Christmas Caroling Outreach. Use one of these ideas for this year's caroling outing:

→ Sing one or two carols at each home within walking distance of the church. Print song sheets for your group so they know the words to sing.

→ Leave a small gift and invitation to worship. Examples: homemade ornament, small Bible with Christmas ribbon, Christmas card signed by carolers.

→ Have the youth group participate in "Kidnap Caroling." As they carol, invite the members of each home to come along for the rest of the party. Add tambourines or sleigh bells. End the caroling at a leader's home for refreshments.

→ Carol at a local nursing home. Have kids make Christmas cards to pass out and plan on staying around to chat for a few minutes after you sing.

→ Begin your Christmas party with "Drive-By Caroling." Decorate cars with battery-operated Christmas lights, wear Christmas hats, and drive slowly through the local mall parking lot, all the nearby fire stations, or other public places to carol. Be sure to obtain permission if needed.

→ Map addresses of children who recently visited or joined your church. Workers wear Christmas hats and use puppets to sing carols at the door.

Knocking Stocking. Fill and personally deliver Christmas stockings to children in needy families. Or make small stockings, add a gift, and invite your children's Sunday School teachers to help deliver them to kids in the church neighborhood.

Disaster Prep. Plan ahead for ministry in your community when disaster occurs. Some churches have a committee or team who researches and makes a plan. Preplanning expedites action. Work with your denomination or disaster relief agency to prepare your church or small group before disaster happens. When a church immediately goes into action, showing God's love during tragedy, He is glorified. It's very effective if everyone wears a church T-shirt. Of course, those who have taken a disaster relief class also wear their credentials. Now, that's a church on mission!

Missionary Mail. Write encouragement letters to missionaries. Get a list from your pastor or church staff of missionaries your church supports.

Random Encouragements. Get a stack of colored index cards and write simple messages of encouragement on them. For example, write, "Good luck studying for finals," on cards, include candy, and pass them out during finals week to students studying in the coffee shop or park.

Welcome Basket Delivery. Deliver a newcomer basket containing community info, a well-designed church brochure, and a small gift to people who are new to town. The gift could be a Bible, a local product, or a handmade item, such as a "God bless this home" plate or "Welcome to [your home town]" ornament. Even better, ask a church member who lives near each new resident to deliver their basket.

Public Picnic. Morph your annual churchwide picnic into a missions event by putting up a banner that says, "Join us for a picnic!" Invite everyone at the park that day to join in—it's not a closed event.

Sky Scripture. Is it springtime? Let's go fly a kite! Head to the dollar store in town and buy 20 kites for $20. Have your family or your small group write "God Loves You" or simple Scriptures on each kite with fat permanent markers. Then, take the kites out to a busy park and invite families who are there to join in on flying the kites. Be ready to strike up a conversation about the Scripture on the kite you are flying.

Kite-Flying Contest. Begin a new citywide tradition to share Christ in a unique way on your church property, a nearby park, or beach. Plan a gigantic first-day-of-spring kite-flying contest. Provide prizes, games, and live music. Assign friendly church members to visit with the crowd and invite each guest to Sunday worship.

Volunteer an Hour. Spend an hour volunteering in your church's benevolence ministry or a local Christian benevolence organization. Your group can accomplish a lot of folding, cleaning, organizing, and serving in an hour!

Pop-Up Popsicles. On a hot day, meet at the city park wearing church T-shirts. Pass out free popsicles to kids, along with printed invitations to Vacation Bible School, kids' camp, or Sunday School. Even better, make it a tradition. People in town never know when that crazy senior adult Popsicle Group will pop up!

GET GOING!
Look with fresh eyes around your community. Discover new ways to live on mission there. See people through the loving eyes of God, and find ways to introduce them to Him.

FOR E-MISSIONS
||||||||||||||||||||||||||

The Internet has exploded with opportunities to reach people in your community and across the nations. How is your church or small group leveraging social media and other online media to reach the people you are connected to online?

Me Inviting You. Make a personal video for an evangelistic event at your church and post it on social media to invite everyone you know to church. Don't know how? Ask a teen in your church to help. Encourage your church members to share the event with all their friends online.

|||||||||||||||

We were having trouble getting people registered for a Christian event in our area. They had done a mailing and email blitz, but that wasn't enough to entice attenders. When we created a Facebook event, however, everyone forwarded it to friends, and attendance was great. Are you using the communication means that your community regularly uses to reach them?

|||||||||||||||

Encourage Devices. Urge church members toward appropriate device usage during worship. Post sermon points, Scripture thoughts, or photos on social media. Link the sermon to the church website. Engage lost friends in the sermon even if they're not there!

Automatic Witness. Add a "missions-purposed" tag line as part of your permanent e-mail signature. This could include a Scripture, quote, or link to an online witnessing tract.

E-Register. Set up Internet registration for every event that guests might attend at your church, such as Vacation Bible School, sports events, addiction group, parenting classes, etc. Can someone who visits your church's website register for a small group online?

Lessen Language Barriers. Take advantage of apps to help you share the gospel in another language. For example, download the 1Cross App (by the Southern Baptists of Texas Convention) for the gospel in every language. Use a translation app. It's a great help for conversations when you don't speak the language.

Mega–E-mail List. Create a large group e-mail list for your church newsletter, special events notices, and e-mails from the pastor. Include every person who visits your worship, kids' camp, Vacation Bible School, sports team, or small groups. Keep them on the list until they ask to be removed. Your outreach will be extended immeasurably.

Like Our Face. Encourage every church member who uses social networking to "like" the church page. They can easily repost events and announcements to their friends.

GET → GOING! Each time you use your computer, ask God to show you ways to share Him online. Be certain that every word on your personal social media honors God and points others to Him.

Screen Saver. Change your personal screensaver at your work, your personal laptop, or phone's home screen to a Scripture or Christian quotation. Follow appropriate office rules, of course. Pray for God to open a door to talk about Him with a friend or co-worker.

Church Website Importance. Create a fantastic website for your church. Keep in mind that most first-time guests who visit your church will look for your church online before they ever walk in your doors. Tell your story with understandable words and excellent photos. Make sure your site reflects your church's heart and purposes.

➡ Hire a web design company if you are able so it can be done with excellence.

➡ Listen to the wisdom of a graphic and web designer for logos, color schemes, fonts, etc.

➡ Many design companies are simply too expensive for some churches to afford. Consider going to your youth or college group and asking for help. Lots of schools these days have assignments for students where they have to do a big project like build a website for a company . . . let their school project be your church site! This makes it a double win: your church gets a fresh website, and the student has the opportunity to be a witness at school with their friends and teachers throughout the project.

➡ Make your church website evangelistic by directing information toward people outside of your church. Have an "I'm New" section of the site that is easy to find, and have the gospel clearly laid out on your site with contact info to follow up with those who visit that page.

➡ Avoid BAEs (bad abbreviation errors). Read and reread every word and update to be assured unchurched people understand. Avoid all acronyms and Christian-ese phrasing. The goal is to attract those who don't know God so they get excited about being a part of what your church is doing. This applies to your weekly church program, too. No bad abbreviation errors.

➡ If your church is in a tourist area, give detailed directions for pedestrians and bus riders on your contact page.

➡ Explore your current church website as if you were someone who doesn't know Jesus. Does its message convey that your church caters not only to believers, but wants to welcome those who aren't yet a Christian?

➡ Be sure your contact information is up to date and checked regularly to follow up with those who visit your site online.

→ Ask a variety of church members to record a video testimony to tell their personal God story.

→ Have an upcoming events area where members and guests can get all the details about the events at your church. Consider linking this to your church's social media account so members can easily invite friends.

FOR CHURCH PLANTER HELP

For a church planter, there's not much that is a greater encouragement than someone else coming in with their actions, prayers, and support. Your encouragement says to us, "I see that God is moving here and I want to be a part of that, even if it's just for a little bit."

Most of these one-hour ideas are for helping a church plant within driving distance of your church. Many, however, could also be used to help a church plant across the country.

Sunday School Substitute. Church plants often have a great need for church workers. Volunteer as a substitute teacher for a Sunday School class or Bible study. This can be especially helpful during summers.

Join their Children's Ministry Team. Serve once a month in the nursery, teach the children's class so all of the church plant's adults can participate in Bible Study, or have your small group adopt their nursery. Send two background-checked adults every Sunday as the church gets started. Offer to pay for the background checks for children and youth workers.

Book Party. Children's books are expensive. Purchase a stack of great bible-centered storybooks for their kids' room.

Love their Kids. Offer to babysit for the planter and his wife so they can have a date night. Or, offer to show up on Sundays to watch their kids while they set up for church and prepare for worship.

Retreat Encouragement. Are they planning a church retreat? Have your church or small group collect an offering to cover all or some of their expenses.

Membership Fees. Pay for the church plant's fee to join the Chamber of Commerce or the pastor's choice of a local service organization or fitness center.

Share Your Blessings. What has God already blessed you with that you can share?

→ Your lake home for a church leadership retreat
→ Your pool for a fellowship
→ Your trailer for transporting supplies
→ Your tent for an event

Borrowed Baptistry. Offer the church planter the use of your church facility for baptisms. Provide towels, hair dryers, and helpers, if needed.

Share Thanks. Invite the new church plant to your church's Thanksgiving dinner. When they arrive, give them special name tags identifying them as a part of the church plant and have your church members go out of their way to encourage and connect with them. Consider spreading those members of the church plant out at different tables so they can share about how God is blessing the work.

Outreach Gift. Purchase boxes of age-appropriate Bibles for the church to give away. Be sure to ask the planter what version of the Bible he would prefer to give away. (Ex. He might like a reader's version of the Bible for school age children, a cool youth Bible with a unique cover to provide youth specific notes and devotions, etc.)

Share Connections. Help with connections and relationships you already have. This can be invaluable to a church planter. Introduce them to politicians, business owners, school principals, bank personnel, accountants, carpenters, etc.

Take a Walk. Do they have an upcoming event? Offer to go around their area and distribute flyers.

Show Up. Be intentional to attend big events the new church plant holds so they have a crowd. While you're there, do whatever they need and focus on sharing Jesus with every person you meet there.

Step Up. Give generously when it's time for the church plant to buy property or begin a new ministry.

Tree Team. Do they have a new building? Purchase flowers and bushes for their landscaping. Get your small group together for a well-planned hour of work, and make the front of their new church beautiful!

Nice Church Brochures. Have your small group all pitch in to cover the printing cost of partnership brochures for the church plant.

The Luxury of a Laminator. Allow them to use your church office equipment. Many church planters would give their right arm for a copier.

Glue and Paper Clips. Do you have a great resource room for craft and office supplies? Offer access to the planter or their children's ministry coordinator to use whatever they need.

GET → GOING! *There's a church planter who could use your church or small group's help and encouragement right now. Don't delay. In less than an hour, you could greatly encourage a church planter.*

Web Matters. Have the skills? Build the church plant a great website!

Software Services. Offer to purchase presentation software for the church plant. (ex. Easy Worship, ProPresenter, etc.)

Graphic Help. Is the church plant in an artsy or modern area? Offer to pay for up-to-date graphic design software (or for a year of subscription-based software) to make their graphics and website top quality.

‖‖‖‖‖‖‖‖‖‖‖‖

My husband and I have a partner church that assigned a person to our church plant. He calls us every few weeks just to ask how we are doing and to pray with us. I don't think I've ever hung up the phone with him without tears in my eyes—and I'm not an emotional girl! It just means so much to physically hear someone praying over you, even on the phone.

‖‖‖‖‖‖‖‖‖‖‖‖

Just Ask. Call or e-mail occasionally to ask how the church planter and his family are doing personally, and also ask about how their work is going. Try to learn all you can about where they are serving. Encourage. Pray. Your interest can be renewing to that church planter.

Watch Out. It's expensive to start something new, and church plants are often overwhelmed by the financial burden that underscores the big dreams in their hearts. Be an encouragement by finding their needs and helping to meet them.

‖‖‖‖‖‖‖‖‖‖‖‖

Our church plant's first building was complete, and some ladies from our sending church threw a baby shower for our church nursery! When they left, it was ready for crowds of babies to arrive. Can you imagine what a great encouragement that was to our new church?

‖‖‖‖‖‖‖‖‖‖‖‖

Befriend a Church Planter's Wife. Make a personal commitment to be her strongest fan and greatest encourager. Take her to lunch. Ask how you can pray for her. Listen well. Send an encouraging letter, email, or text. Share a good book. Help enhance her joy in ministry. For example, if she cares deeply about reaching teens, contribute money from your own garage sale to help with a youth event.

Big Events. If they're just getting started, invite them to join in on your church's Christmas Eve or Good Friday services. Give people in their church ownership in the service. Ask them to pray, serve on the greeting team, read Scripture, or be on the worship team with your leaders.

See a Need. Donate gently used equipment for their worship service.

Are They a Mobile Church? Mobile churches have unique needs that you might not be thinking about. For example, they can't have baby cribs, or they probably don't have permanent signage. Storage might even be an issue for the supplies they use regularly. You can help by gifting needed supplies or services that they might not have the funding to purchase:

→ Offering plates or baskets
→ Offering envelopes
→ Communion supplies
→ Laptop for the pastor or projection in Sunday worship services
→ Portable cribs and changing pads (instead of cribs and changing tables)
→ Age-appropriate toys (be sure they are easy to transport)
→ Large rolling containers or tubs for supplies to be transported or stored
→ Craft supplies for children's ministry (crayons, markers, glue, colored paper, coloring books, etc.)
→ Pens with their church logo and website
→ Offer to cover the monthly rental fee for their storage facility.

→ Just show up! Getting started is difficult. As a planter, they are inviting tons of people to a church that may or may not even have a core group that attends yet. You can be a body in a seat that gives the plant that irreducible minimum to not have the service feel awkward when a visitor arrives.

→ Make baked goods for church each week.

⚊⚊⚊⚊⚊⚊

When we started our church in Indianapolis, my mom baked a plate of homemade goodies for our welcome table every week. Having a homemade brownie or Rice Krispies treat in their hands made every visitor glad they showed up!

⚊⚊⚊⚊⚊⚊

Creative Funding. Organize a garage sale to fund a project the new church plant wants to do.

Generous Gifts. Gift the planter with an extravagant gift card to a nice restaurant in town. Even better, join them, and let them talk about their church plant for the entire dinner.

Sponsor a Planter. Scholarship the planter and his wife to attend a conference they are dying to go to. Consider making it a scholarship for four, so they can take another couple from their plant, too. Are they taking seminary classes? Purchase their books for the next semester.

⚊⚊⚊⚊⚊⚊

Diana and Steve were church planters. Autumn and Yale are currently church planters. Every church where we've both served has planted other churches. From our personal experience, we assure you that your encouragement will make a huge impact on a church planter.

⚊⚊⚊⚊⚊⚊

After-Share. Is your church's women's ministry doing a video Bible study? When you finish, pass the DVDs and books on to the church plant to use. Is their VBS scheduled after yours? Offer decor and extra materials. You might even share a VBS teacher or two.

FOR INTERNATIONAL MISSIONARIES
IIIIIIIIIIIIIIIIIIIIIIIIIIIIIIIIIIIIIIIIIIIIIIIIIIIIIIII

Get creative with ideas of how your church or small group can do missions by encouraging a missionary you support. We'll have more in the next sections, but here are a few ways you can do that in just an hour:

Group Gift. Prepare a package for an overseas missionary. Have your Sunday School class gather items that may not be available overseas, such as mac-and-cheese or candies, along with encouraging notes, homemade cookies, and a newly released worship CD. Box up the items and mail them to a missionary serving in a foreign country. As a group, commit to pray for that missionary every week as you gather to study the Bible. Shipping will cost some money, so have everyone pitch in a few dollars.

Read and Respond. When a missionary sends a newsletter or e-report, read it thoroughly and respond in some way. Watch for needs and meet them. Pray faithfully and tell them! As you read a missionary's social media post, click "like" or comment. Ask God to prompt you and help you to meet practical needs you read about in their newsletters.

Pray for the Nations Night. Have a night focused on prayer for the nations. This could be done as a one-hour come-and-go event.

→ Set up an open space with flags from multiple countries as decor.

→ Have an artist in the church make a massive map of the world on the floor with masking tape and invite people to stand on a country as they pray for the people who live there.

→ Have videos, photos, testimonies, and prayer points for specific countries so people know how to pray effectively.

→ Need help with prayer points? Check out operationworld.org for updated statistics and prayer needs.

→ Have live music playing and give people direction for what to do and how to pray.

Care Call. Does your church have a partnership with a missionary or church planter overseas? Ask permission from the church staff to call or video chat with the missionary to encourage and pray for them. Ask how their ministry is going and how you can pray for them. Inquire about their family's adjustment to the missions field and who the people are they are ministering to. When you pray with them over the phone, pray specifically for the needs they mentioned.

Know How to Pray. Research what is going on in the world today. Instead of only reading/watching local news, go to another country's news website and read their perspective of world events. Ask God to show you ways to pray for the nations of the earth.

Offer Your Expertise. Find out needs that you can meet through your personal skill set. Contact a missionary your church supports and offer to help for an hour a week for the next year. (This could also be done for a church planter.) Whatever your profession, hobby, or skill set—it can be used for the glory of God. Figure out how!

→ Are you a realtor? Offer to help them find property.

→ Are you a financial consultant? Offer to assist their finance team in building a church budget.

→ Are you a wood worker? Offer to build them a pulpit they help design.

→ Are you a graphic or web designer? Offer to build a website or create sermon series graphics or invitation cards.

→ Are you a Sunday School teacher? Offer training in person or over video chat with their children's workers to share your experience.

→ Are you good with the computer? Offer to put together or design their weekly worship program or monthly newsletter.

Remember Regularly. Read their website, social media, or e-newsletter for the church planters or missionaries your church supports. Click "like" or reply with a one-line encouragement.

Support a Missions Trip Participant. Is your youth or college group going on a missions trip? Donate extravagantly to the team fund as they work to raise support for their trip.

Birthday Blessing. Distribute attractive prayer reminder cards with the name of a missionary whose birthday is that day (from Missions Mosaic, a publication of national Woman's Missionary Union®). This takes work, but people will pray! Ask all members of your group to sign a birthday a card to a specific missionary.

GET→GOING!

As you serve where God has placed you, don't forget to encourage vocational missionaries across the nation and the world.

FOR YOUR COMMUNITY LEADERS

Some leaders in your community may not know God personally. Will you take an hour to impact them for Christ? Try one of these ideas.

Badge Bibles. Purchase policemen's or firemen's Bibles and deliver them to the community station. Be sure to write on the inside that you are praying for them and include your church's web address.

Prayer Promise. Look on your town's website and find a list of city council representatives or other leaders. Write individual notes of sincere appreciation for their work, and commit to pray for them faithfully. Write out 1 Timothy 2:1–2, add a photo of your whole group holding a giant "we are praying for you" sign, and include an invitation to church in your note.

GET → GOING!

Get to know leaders in your community and pray faithfully for them. God may use you to help them meet the God of the universe.

Unique Fire Gift. Deliver a stack of new board games to the local fire station with a bow and an encouragement note letting them know that your church/small group is praying for them as they serve.

Prayers and Politics. Before voting day, each small group selects one elected position. Purchase a nice Bible, highlight favorite Scriptures, and write an encouraging note in the front promising prayer. Deliver it to the official elected to that office immediately after the election.

Food for Thought. Deliver snack baskets to local fire stations, police stations, highway patrol headquarters, and the mayor's office. Be sure snacks are store-bought and sealed. Include personal notes of prayer and encouragement. Add a church brochure and give a verbal invitation when you deliver.

FOR YOUR OWN NEIGHBORS

You live there. Your neighborhood is your missions field, too. Do you know their names? Do you know their kids or their pets? It's easy to live next door and never share more than a smile and a wave, but Jesus said to love our neighbors—how good are you at doing that? Take an hour and try one of these easy ideas to impact the people who live around you.

Pizza Is Love. Keep a small stack of gift cards to the local pizza company that delivers to your neighborhood. When you notice a new neighbor moving in on your street, take them a gift card along with a welcome note and the phone number to call and order pizza. No one wants to cook when they're moving in. Or, keep brownie mix and icing in your pantry, and deliver warm brownies. Your welcome note should include your personal e-mail, phone number, and address, along with an invitation to your church or small group.

Mow for Jesus. Mowing your yard this Saturday? Take an extra hour and mow your neighbor's yard, too!

Small Group in Lawn Chairs. Have a small group that meets in your home? Plan to meet this summer in your front yard instead of your living room. Order a yard sign that says, "[Our Church] Small Group meets here. Join us today at 7 p.m." and put it in the yard on your meeting day. Have members of your small group all bring extra lawn chairs so there's plenty of space for new people to join in.

Soup Ingredients. Take a trip to the grocery to stock canned ingredients for your favorite soup, and include bottled water, crackers, plastic spoons, and bowls. Set everything aside in storage. When an ice storm, tornado, or other crisis hits your neighborhood, start cooking immediately. Then walk through the neighborhood to invite neighbors for food.

Bake and Deliver. Share cookies with your neighbors on the first or last day of school.

Walk around the Block. Speak to every neighbor who's outside. Eventually you'll learn their names, their dog's name, etc. Pray as you walk, and ask God to provide conversations that lead to a personal witness.

Be Neighborly. Watch closely for opportunities to serve neighbors. Help carry groceries, sign for a package, step in during crisis situations, share soup on a snowy day, send a sympathy note, give a lift to the airport, begin a neighborhood Bible study, and be a friend. Opportunities to share Christ will follow.

GET → GOING!

Every time you walk out of your dorm room, apartment building, or front door, breathe a prayer for your neighborhood/missions field. Be intentional about shining for Christ there.

Traveling Tea Party. Fill a basket with a thermos of hot water, teabags, napkins, cookies, and two teacups. Take it to your elderly next-door neighbor's home and serve tea with great flourish while you chat about what God is doing in your life.

Extra Sweet. Deliver baked goods to your neighbor who has small children. Learn their names while you're there, and commit to pray for them.

Neighbor Gift. Make stepping stones for your neighbors. Use pizza boxes and a bag of concrete. Pour the concrete into the pizza box and use a trowel to even off the top. Use marbles, broken tiles, or other small trinkets to spell out "God Loves You" or part of your favorite Scripture on the top of the concrete. Let it set until hardened completely. Then, cut away the pizza box, and deliver with a smile to your neighbor.

Sidewalk Chalk Your Neighborhood. Take your family or small group and go around your neighborhood drawing fun pictures and writing encouraging notes on the sidewalks with chalk. As you draw, pray for every home. As people stop you to ask what you're doing, share the love of Jesus.

FOR EVERYDAY LIFE
||||||||||||||||||||||||||||||||

Hebrews 10:24 instructs Christians: "Let us think of ways to motivate one another to acts of love and good works." God may not be calling you today to move to another region—but He is calling you today to be on mission wherever you are. Try some of these simple ways to spend an hour living on mission during everyday life.

Garage Sale Missionary. Do you love going to garage sales? Be a garage sale missionary! Visit garage sales as you usually do, but be intentional about inviting the host to your church, offering to pray for him or her.

The 52 Challenge. Members commit to personally invite one person— friend or stranger—to church every week this year, and write the names on a group calendar in your small group classroom so everyone can pray for them.

In Your Face. Add a Scripture card somewhere on your car dashboard. Ask God to use it to give you opportunities to share Him with your passengers.

> *So beginning with this same Scripture, Philip told him the Good News about Jesus.* —Acts 8:35

Appreciate a Service Provider. Make an intentional, ongoing plan to offer kindness and an invitation to your church every time a worker comes to your church (or home)—a plumber, electrician, carpet installer, pest control professional, and so on. If the repair is large, such as a new roof, prepare a nice lunch for the entire crew one day. For example, your class, church, or team could prepare treat bags labeled with, "Thank you for serving our church," containing a bottled water, snack, and handwritten note inviting the repairman to come to worship on Sunday. Include a church brochure and witnessing tract. The person in the church office who interacts with the workers can present the gift bag and give a verbal invitation.

Watch for Road Crews. Keep a case of bottled water ready. If there's a construction crew across the street or a road crew working near your church, deliver water and a snack. Be sure to invite them for Sunday worship.

A Novel Witness. Share a great Christian novel with a friend. Ask them to call you when they finish so you can chat.

Military Missions. Mail two military Bibles to a church member who is deployed, and suggest that he or she share the extra one with a friend who needs a relationship with Jesus.

Military Mail. Help deployed church members be a witness. Prepare a goodie box with plenty to share, and include notes of prayer from your small group or church.

Hobbies for Him. If a few members are involved in the same hobby, how can they be "on mission"? For example, if a few run marathons, others in the church could wear church T-shirts as they volunteer at a water table or cheer at the finishing line. A few folks in our singles small group rode bicycles in a bike club. They interacted regularly in person and in the group's online chat room, discussing life questions and responding with God's love and Scripture. When a cyclist was killed in a bike accident, the ministry opportunities exploded. Because they already saw their hobby as a mission for Christ, God used them in great ways. What's your hobby?

> *When I am with those who are weak, I share their weakness, for I want to bring the weak to Christ. Yes, I try to find common ground with everyone, doing everything I can to save some. I do everything to spread the Good News and share in its blessings. Don't you realize that in a race everyone runs, but only one person gets the prize? So run to win!* —1 Corinthians 9:22–24

Envelope Idea. Ask each member of your small group or church to put $20 (or $5 or $100) in an envelope in his or her pocket. Include a note that reads, "Remember that God loves you," and a card with your church's website and information. Ask God to give you direction, and discretely give it to someone you meet who has a need. Share stories of how God works through the project.

On the Job Missionary. Whether you work in the executive office, the mail room, the farm, the factory or the pharmacy, you are an ambassador for God there. Make a renewed commitment to God to be His missionary at work. Live intentionally as you work. Listen at the water cooler for needs, and find ways you can respond to them. As you live intentionally for Him, you'll find co-workers asking you to pray for them. You'll see opportunities to converse about the difference God can make.

Dual-Purpose Party. Plan your child's birthday party with lost friends in mind. Yes, invite church friends, but include friends who don't know Jesus. Take time during the party to pray over your child in front of the group and celebrate the things God has done in his or her life the last year.

Pocket Witness. Keep witnessing tracts on hand. Give them out to drive-through cashiers, policeman when they stop you for a ticket, homeless people, or the drive-through pharmacist. Tell them that this is something very important in your life, and you want to share it with them. Next time you see that person, ask what they thought of the tract.

Daily Notes. Subscribe to the local newspaper or a local e-news service. Prepare a basket of stamped envelopes, your favorite witnessing tracts, brochures and business cards for your church, and keep the basket near where you read the news. Send a few notes each day as God prompts to congratulate, offer prayer, or encourage.

Guest Follow Up. Volunteer to spend an hour on Sunday afternoons to call or e-mail first-time guests to your church. Pick up their contact information after worship, then call each one to thank them for coming and answer their questions.

Delivery Friends. Be sure to regularly thank the mail carrier and delivery person who serves your church. Assign a specific person or team to learn their names, and prepare occasional thank you notes, treats, and personal invitations to worship at your church. For example, wrap a good pair of gloves as a Christmas gift.

Christian at College. Find out the name and address of church members who've gone away to college. Prepare a triple portion box of homemade cookies and treats, and mail it to the student with a promise of prayer. Encourage the student to share the treats with a roommate and friends who may not know Christ.

GET GOING! Every step you take through life reveals more opportunities to live on mission for Him. Get Going!

ONE-DAY MISSIONS IDEAS

Each day proclaim the good news that he saves.
—Psalm 96:2

ot a little more time and want a bigger project? These ideas take a bit more planning and preparation and are great for your church or small group to use as a missions project. Plan ahead. Advertise well. Train the people involved to share the gospel with people you serve. Plan a Saturday service day together and choose an idea in this section. Or, let these ideas spur on another even better idea that will be perfect for your group—just do something!

FOR THE COMMUNITY

It's amazing what a well-planned one-day project can accomplish in your community. Try one of these ideas:

1-2-3 Serve! Each small group in the church plans and implements a servant evangelism project on the same Saturday, blitzing the entire community with good works in Jesus' name. Each group plans their own missions project. Projects may be done for the community or for people outside the church. Each team sends photos in real time by cell phone and reports results. Print brightly colored church T-shirts, and people in your city will definitely notice. You'll find lots of ideas in the one-hour Chapter, but here are a few starters: Clean a neighborhood lot or street corner that has become an eyesore. Cook hot dogs in the city park and give them away. Feed a meal to the homeless. Paint a school playground. One group even cleared a historic, densely over-grown cemetery and had opportunities to witness to several neighbors.

You've Been gLOVEd. As a Christmas project, ask members to collect gloves of all sizes. Make cards that say, "You have been gLOVEd by [our church]," place the notes inside each pair, then roll the gloves like socks. As members bring them to your church, use ornament hooks or ribbon to attach the rolled-up gloves to a Christmas tree in the church lobby. Once the collection is over, go outside to a park, street corner, or college campus to pass them out as a small group, or donate them to a school or your local benevolence ministry.

Drive-Through Prayer. Is your church property near a school or busy intersection? During the first week of school or finals weeks, set up signs advertising a drive-through prayer. Have plenty of church mem-bers of all ages ready to voice a quick prayer with students and parents and hand out a printed flyer inviting them to your church's children's or youth ministries. Be sure to make it quick—no one likes sitting in a drive-through forever. Make it your goal for every car to be stopped for three minutes or less.

||||||||||||||||

Believe me, the whole town took notice. Every small group in our church planned a servant ministry-type project for our community on the same Saturday. Happy people, in brightly colored church T-shirts, were everywhere in town! They served hot dogs in the park, cleared overgrown lots, fed the hungry, painted school playground equipment, cleaned up the city sign, hosted block parties, and lots more. They had fun, made a difference, and showed God's love to those around them.

||||||||||||||||

Give Something Away. Set up a drive-through lane in your church parking lot with a large sign. Keep the line moving as cars drive through for their free treat. The purpose is to do something nice for the community as an evangelistic tool. Have fun and love people. Watch for ways to chat about God, and personally invite each individual to church. Do not accept contributions at all. With the free item, include a small card inviting them to church on Sunday. This can be as simple as teens serving snow cones as cars drive through or a Valentine's Day cookie giveaway. You can give away:

→ Snow cones
→ Windshield washes
→ Cotton candy
→ Short, upbeat Christian songs
→ Bibles or New Testaments
→ Popcorn
→ Hot chocolate or coffee on a cold day
→ Lemonade or soft drinks on a hot day
→ Prayers
→ Frisbees, imprinted with church logo

Bubble Mania. Every kid loves bubbles. Invest in as many bubble machines and toys you can find, and buy some of the large bottles of bubble refills. Take all of this out to your neighborhood park or field, and hold a bubble party for any kid at the park that day. While they play with bubbles, be intentional about investing in them. Ask them questions that will make them think about Jesus. Tell them a story from the Bible, and share the gospel in an age-appropriate way. Are parents there, too? Have people focused on sharing with the parents as well and be sure to have invite cards for your church with you. Who can resist playing with bubbles in the summer?

College Move-In Day. Get permission from your local university to bring a large team to help move freshmen into their new dorms on move-in day.

➡ Print brightly colored T-shirts for your team to wear, identifying your church name, website, and, "We love college students. See you Sunday!"

➡ Have some sort of a small gift for the students you move in—a pen or folder with church logo, etc.

➡ Print small magnets with your church's website on them and put one on every mini-fridge you move.

➡ Have the whole church donate bottles of water to give out to students and family members as they move.

➡ Don't forget the campus residence hall staff! Be an encouragement to them. This can be a very stressful day for their team.

➡ Go above and beyond by offering to take trash to the Dumpster, sweep and mop up the lobby at the end of the day, or buy a stack of pizzas for tired staff.

➡ Work hard. Work with joy. They'll notice.

➡ As you move students into their dorms, present each student with an info card about your church's college ministry and a token gift. Examples: A pen or lanyard with your church logo.

➡ At the end of the day, gather your move-in crew to share stories of students they met and pray together for the ones they moved in.

→ Consider sending a team of people back to the dorm lobbies that evening with board games and snacks. Get to know the students and help them acclimate to their new home.

→ Offer to stop by and pick up students who would like a ride to your church on Sunday. Be ready on Sunday with a great Bible class and free lunch.

→ Make a pile of homemade cookies and deliver to the dorm foyers with another invitation to church a week later.

Street Art. Have artists in your church? Send them out to a crowded area of town and have them set up their easels and paint or draw. Give them a missional theme (ex. God's heart for the nations, character of God, God's love, etc.) and a stack of cards for your church, and have them watch for opportunities to share

Make a Difference. Select a street in your community that is in disrepair. Gather a group from your church to have a big one-day project day on that street. Pull all of the weeds, edge the sidewalks, and clean graffiti. Wear your church T-shirts, and don't forget to knock on every door, introduce yourselves, and distribute invitations to join your small group or church worship service.

> *Suppose you see a brother or sister who has no food or clothing, and you say, "Good-bye and have a good day; stay warm and eat well"—but then you don't give that person any food or clothing. What good does that do? So you see, faith by itself isn't enough. Unless it produces good deeds, it is dead and useless.* —James 2:15–17

Food Fight. Collect food for your benevolence ministry. Designate the fifth Sunday for food collection. Or distribute a list of needed items. Or make it a contest between small groups.

||||||||||||||||

Every year growing up our youth group at church held a massive food fight in early November. No, we didn't throw food—it was a fight between the grade levels to see who could donate the most food to our church's benevolence ministry. We planned ahead to get donations to accomplish our goal of 20,000 pounds of food every year. Not only did we have some friendly competition, we also stocked the church's food pantry for Thanksgiving and months to come.

||||||||||||||||

Community Kids' Stuff Swap. Have church members and community members bring items (clothing, shoes, sporting gear) that their kids have outgrown or no longer need to swap with things their kids do need. Instruct church members to be generous in what they bring and to not take anything home! This is strictly a ministry to the church neighborhood. Send every family home with an invitation to your next kid's ministry event or class.

Bring the Kids. Have a great hill by your church? Turn it into a sledding hill for the neighborhood in the winter season! Tie a long rope to a pole at the top of the hill to help children climb up easier. Be sure your insurance liability policy is up to date. Remember that the goal is to include neighbors and get to know them.

Cardboard Works. Live in a state with no snow? There's a solution for that hill! Purchase some large blocks of ice and some dollar-store towels, and use the block of ice as a sled to glide down a grassy hill. Or use big pieces of cardboard for a sledding race.

Free Engagement Photos. Got photographers in your church? Register couples in your community for free engagement photos! As you spend the afternoon with them taking photos, use the opportunity to invest in them and be sure you invite them to get connected to your church's nearly-wed class or growing young couple's ministry.

Drive-Through VBS Registration. In the most visible part of your church parking lot, set up a one-day, eye-catching registration booth for your church's upcoming Vacation Bible School. The young single adult class did this as a missions project in our church. Have fun as you register lots of children who may not know Jesus.

Ramp Experts. Pay attention to needs of the elderly in your community. Create a team of builders from your church who can install handicap ramps at their homes, and ask church members to offer the service to people they know who need one. While there, offer to change light bulbs or smoke alarm batteries for them. Share the good news about Jesus.

Christmas with Children in Need. Children's Group Homes and juvenile detention facilities are great places to take your small group on Christmas Day. Take gifts for the kids and supplies to make gingerbread houses together. Talk with the manager to discover long-term ways your church could be involved in ministry there.

Beach Outreach. Live near a beach? Head out this weekend with bags full of bottled water, floatable foam tubes, and inflatable rafts from the dollar store. Acquire travel-size tubes of sunscreen. As you walk up and down the beach praying for your community, distribute water, sunscreen, and toys as you see a need. Live near a ski lodge? A recreational lake? A tourist attraction? Brainstorm ways you can be on mission there.

Father's Day Grill-Out. Have everyone in your small group bring their grill from home and set up outside the church building. Post an outdoor sign inviting the whole community to bring their dad for lunch. Ask different small groups to provide meat, side items, and desserts. Have children's workers bring supplies for a Father's Day craft that the kids can make to give to dad.

Pet Photos. Have a citywide pet photo day. Gather all of your church photographers, and set up several themed sets where people can pose with their animals. Make it free and request their e-mail addresses. Then, send the images via e-mail. Or, promise a printed copy on Sunday at church.

New Mommy's Tea. Every six months, plan a lovely, fun tea for new moms in your community, with a focus on church members bringing moms who are unchurched. Provide tours of the church nursery, and have the regular nursery workers in the rooms to meet them. Print invitations for church members to give to new mothers they know and an e-invitation so members can forward to new moms. Request RSVPs for child care and attendance. Provide time for new moms to ask questions of seasoned moms as well as time to simply connect with each other. Have moms in your church each host a table of new moms to be the "expert" encourager, to connect with guests, or even lead discussion if the need should arise.

Kids' Day Trips as Outreach. Give your kids' day trips a missional focus by asking every kid to invite their friends, particularly their friends who don't go to church. Kids who bring a friend get to go first in line. Ask for discounts at the local zoo, water park, or children's museum to keep the cost low. Have plenty of adult supervision, and make it lots of fun. As they leave, give each child a list of family and children events at your church.

Missions Scavenger Hunt. Here's a twist on the traditional scavenger hunt. Teams follow a map that prompts them to perform various ministry projects. Plan well to provide needed tools and materials. Make it a fun and fruitful afternoon, giving everyone a great taste of missions action.

Christian Cool in Middle School. Prep your incoming middle school students and their parents. Rotate them through ten-minute topical classes taught by church youth leaders and Christians who teach or work in local middle schools. Have a panel of Christian eighth graders to answer questions that incoming students have about student life. Provide information about your church's youth ministry as well as other ministries students can get involved in at your local school (ex. Fellowship of Christian Athletes, See You at the Pole, etc.) Afterward, host a party for all the middle school students in your church, and provide a meal for the parents. Make the event into a missions project by asking friends and their parents to join.

Wall of Veggies. Collecting food for benevolence? Consider challenging the church to build a giant wall of Spam, or a mountain of macaroni. Plan a way to safely display the collection.

Minister to the Local High School. Talk with a church member who works on staff, and ask for a "wish list" of things that might make a difference at the school. Those who work there may know special needs that your small group or church can meet. For example, if the golf team has a long trip coming up, you could prepare snack bags. Take up a collection in your small group, assign a team, include a note from the group or the pastor, and an invitation to come to church.

Get Disaster Ready. Evangelism and missions flow naturally from disaster relief ministry, but you must personally be credentialed to volunteer in major disaster situations. The training is usually a day long and may be available through your local denominational office. Take disaster relief training now so you can be a missionary in your own community when crisis occurs. Disaster relief opportunities often include mass feedings, chaplains to pray, emergency response teams, temporary child care services, spiritual care, emotional help, cleanup and recovery, and administrative support. There are often mud-out teams, all types of construction work, and other volunteer work.

Video Interviews. Film random people around your town answering a question that goes along with your next sermon series. Have your church videographer edit together a quick video for use before the sermon as a bonus for your church. The real purpose here is to get into conversations with individuals about Jesus. Take every opportunity to share the gospel with each person your team encounters. You could even invite those on the video to come to worship to see themselves.

GET → GOING! *What's unique about your community? Discover how God can use your small group or church to share His name there.*

See a Need. Pick It Up. Look around your community and see the needs. Get permission, if needed, and meet the need. (Note: This is not "social ministry." It's community missions. It's missional evangelism.) Examples:

→ Inquire about cleanup or repair needs at your local school facilities.
→ Clean landscape around the city sign.
→ Paint playground equipment at a school or park.
→ Edge the sidewalks all down the street.
→ Clean up an overgrown or trashed street corner.

Purposeful Garage Sale-ing. Collect money in your small group for a few weeks. On a good weather Saturday, go garage sale shopping and get lots of great stuff. Deliver the items to your church's halfway house or to a needy family in your area. Keep a family in mind as you do this— do they really need a couch? Or a bed for their kids' room? Only buy things you would put in your own home, and deliver them with the love of Jesus.

Street Party. A well-planned block party can be a successful way to impact a neighborhood. Our church launched each of our apartment ministries with a block party.

Participate. If your community already does a big family-friendly fall event for kids, participate in that instead of putting on your own. Have multiple groups in your church each purchase a booth space and provide multiple places for families to connect with your church.

Visible Improvement. Select a prime street corner near your church or in a needy area of town. Plan a day-long project of cleanup, landscape, and beautification. If there is graffiti, ask the police department if you can help remove it.

Truckers and Travelers. If you're located near a truck stop or airport, consider a plan to minister in Jesus' name to stranded truckers or travelers during a weather crisis

FOR THE CHURCH NEIGHBORHOOD

People in the community around your church building need Jesus. These one-day projects could make a difference.

Skaters Welcome. Entice local kids who skateboard to attend youth Bible study by building a rack to hold skateboards. Even better, build a full skate park in your church parking lot and love them to Jesus. Be sure to update church liability insurance.

Church Neighborhood Coffee. Get to know the people who live nearest your church building. Map a specific area nearest your church, such as a one-block radius, two-block radius, or neighborhood surrounding the church. Limit to a doable number. Plan a nice, relaxed coffee before or after a worship service, and mail and/ or personally deliver an invitation to each home the week ahead. Make it great! Use name tags. Lots of friendly church members mingle to meet, learn needs and personally invite guests to worship.

Church Neighbor Day. Do a personal delivery invitation to every neighbor who lives within a few blocks of the church, inviting him or her to worship and to a "neighborhood coffee" (on previous page) on a specific Sunday. The coffee could be before or after worship. Provide name tags, snacks, and lots of friendly church members to embrace them. Their assignment: listen carefully to learn needs and names, sit with them in worship, and personally invite each guest to a small group or church event. Designate a special assigned seating area to recognize and welcome them as a group.

Love Your Neighbor Day. Designate a Sunday and encourage every church member to bring an unchurched neighbor.

HOA Meets Here. Offer your building to be used for annual meetings of nearby Homeowner Associations. Do it well, and if it's necessary to charge a fee, make it very minimal. This is a great time to practice hospitality.

➡ Have a team of people from your church on hand to serve the group.

➡ Serve homemade snacks as they arrive.

➡ Set up the room the way they need it and clean up afterward.

➡ Place a welcome crew at every door of the building to hold doors and give directions.

➡ Provide child care.

➡ If they like the idea, your pastor or another staff minister could say a greeting to the group before they begin.

➡ Let your walls do the "talking" about upcoming events and welcoming newcomers.

Company Connections. Work to create great relationships with businesses around your church building. Consider ways to support and encourage the owners and employees. Make a list of every business located near your church—restaurant, insurance office, dry cleaners, etc. Be a good neighbor to them. Put them on your church newsletter list. "Like" them on social media. Make intentional plans to show that you care. Ask your Sunday School class to use the car wash across the street on a particular day. The day before, send a note from the pastor or class leader letting them know your class will be supporting them that day. If possible, have every car sport a church bumper sticker. Have one person stop to meet the manager and leave a church brochure. If there is a service company, such as a carpet cleaner, try to use them for church business.

||||||||||||||||

A small group in our church spent an hour one Sunday afternoon visiting homes near our church building. They enjoyed meeting church neighbors and asked how our church could pray for them. One man had just discovered he had cancer, so the group prayed faithfully and ministered to him during his recovery.

||||||||||||||||

Neighborhood Newsletter. If nearby neighborhoods have a neighborhood newsletter or e-newsletter, ask if they would mind publishing an announcement for your church (their neighbor). Select only one thing for each newsletter, and warmly invite the neighborhood to come. It should be an event or specific ministry that might reach unchurched people. Examples: fall festival for children, singles retreat, free garage sale, benevolence ministry (food, clothing, interview help, etc.), Bible class about finances, parenting, marriage, a community garden, or English as a Second Language or GED classes.

Clean Inside and Out. If there are homeless or needy people in your church neighborhood, and if your church has a shower facility, consider opening the showers for them to use once a week. Provide soaps, shampoos, and towels, and treat them graciously.

Visible at Voting. Volunteer your church as a voting site for upcoming elections. Make your building and entrance area as attractive as possible. Be intentional to use entry area walls to tell about great things happening at church and invite newcomers. Remember: every person who votes there is a neighbor, and many of them need Christ. Church members who volunteer at the polls can request to work at the church site. Plan a snack for the polling volunteers, and be sure the pastor or other leaders stop by to meet them and invite them to church.

Meet at Church. Joyfully share your church facilities for appropriate community events. For example, the public school can use your nicest classrooms for teacher training events. The fellowship hall or gym might be loaned for school banquets. See this as a missions opportunity, and treat the guests well when they arrive.

GET → GOING!
The Great Commission challenge from Jesus begins where we are and extends to the world. Don't overlook those who live right around your church facility.

Neighborly News. If your church is located in a residential neighborhood, watch for ways to use mail to help create a relationship. If you mail church newsletters, add those nearby to the mailing list. Send flyers about major outreach events they might enjoy. A small group could make a project of handwriting a neighborly note to each resident, perhaps inviting them to join them for small group on a specific date.

Apartment Impact. Be intentional about ministering in apartment complexes. Select a specific apartment complex, maybe even one near your church, and make an impact for Christ there.

→ Encourage a church member to move into an apartment complex, and get permission from the manager to minister to neighbors.

→ Use the facilities of the complex as much as you are allowed for outreach.

→ Plan a pool party, and have your church youth and children's leaders present to connect with families with you.

→ Work out in the gym at your complex at the same time every day, and get to know the people in there at that time. Make friends. Share Jesus!

→ Ask a financially minded person at your church to host a financial seminar in the clubhouse of your complex to help residents get out of debt—with Christ at the center.

→ Get permission to have a youth or children's game night or movie night in the party room or gym. Invite a children's or youth class from your church to participate with the intention of inviting and integrating those from the apartment into their class.

→ If you have a playground or field in your complex, host an Easter egg hunt, cookout, or flag football game.

→ Get permission from the main office to go door-to-door inviting people in your complex to your church. Provide a printed invitation with your e-mail address or the church's main phone number on it saying, "Call/E-mail me if you need a ride!"

→ As you get to know people, consider beginning a small group Bible study in the church member's apartment or home of another volunteer.

New to Town. Have an apartment complex adjacent to your church? Schedule "new to town parties" throughout the year for new residents. Ask permission to host the event at the apartment's clubhouse (or at your church facility). Prepare packets that include information about the community, coupons, a list of church classes and events, and an invitation to church. Or plan the welcome event in the church fellowship hall, and invite every new resident within a few blocks, using newcomer lists.

FOR CHURCH PLANTERS/MISSIONARIES

Do you live in a large city? It is very likely that there are multiple church planters all around you. Have you found a way to be an encouragement to the church planters in your area or across the world? It doesn't take a lot of time, but even just taking a day to be an encouragement to their ministry could mean the world to not only their church plant, but also to their hearts personally. Consider using one of these ideas to take a bit of time to be an encouragement and strength to missionaries all around you.

One Vacation Day. Get the contact info for a church planter near where you're vacationing, and arrange ahead of time to meet him for coffee, take his family to dinner, or help with a one-day project they already have scheduled. Encourage. Listen. Pray.

Shower the Plant. The church plant, that is. When the church plant that your church sponsors opens its first building, host a huge kitchen shower or nursery shower. Make a specific list of every possible item they may need, and supply it beautifully. Then volunteer to staff the nursery on the first Sunday. If the church is in another state or country, ship the gifts. Alternate ideas:

→ Landscape shower: trees, plants, mulch, and teams to plant it all

→ A/V shower: gift all their audio and video equipment

→ Kid's ministry shower: games, books, and decor items for kids' rooms

→ Youth shower: game room supplies, bean bags, Bibles

→ Sanctuary shower: offering envelopes, communion supplies, Bibles, decor items, a pulpit or lectern

Or do all of the ideas above, with a different class or group sponsoring each theme. Be sure you ask the church planter for a detailed wish list.

One-Day Survey. Volunteer your small group to spend a day doing a survey for your church plant that's within driving distance. The planter should dictate the questions they want you to ask in their community that will help direct their ministry in the area.

Crowd in the Driveway. If your church plant is within driving distance, consider welcoming the church planter's family when they move there. Recruit a small crowd to welcome their moving van and help them move in. Show support and excitement about their response to God's call, and commit to pray for them.

Advertising Assistance. One of the most challenging parts of planting a church is letting people know you are there. Help a local church planter or missionary out by offering your small group to go door-to-door handing out flyers inviting people in the neighborhood to worship on Sunday. Or, offer to go do some investigative work, finding community boards in your area where the church can regularly post information about worship services and events. The planter will be thrilled to have this list!

||||||||||||||

As we were starting our church plant in downtown Indianapolis, our friend who lived downtown made a list of all the available community boards. Grocery stores, coffee shops, even the local bar would allow us to put up a flyer to advertise an event or service for the community! Even now, a few years later, we have a team of people who take that list and go around to each place with a flyer every few weeks to keep our presence in the community updated.

||||||||||||||

Administrative Assistance. Offer a missionary or church planter a day of your help with any administrative needs. The best thing about this is that you can often do many administrative tasks from far away. That means you don't have to have a church planter in your town to serve them in this way. You can create visitor packets for a church plant in Toronto or San Francisco! You can make phone calls to visitors, print bulletins for Sunday's worship service, research curriculum, search online for needed supplies and create a digital shopping cart for them, make copies, or put together first-time visitor packets. These things take a lot of time—time that a planter usually doesn't have an abundance of. Even better, offer to give a day's administrative help once a week for a year.

GET → GOING!

Your church or small group could make all the difference for a church planter and the future of that new church.

Discipleship. Visit the missionary or planter's ministry and get to know people they serve in their city. When you make a connection with someone in their ministry, offer to meet with them to encourage them in their personal walk with God. This could be in person, over the phone, or on a video chat of some sort. Be sure you are communicating well with the planter/missionary so they can give you context for this discipleship.

FOR COMMUNITY EVENTS

When a church is positively involved in the community, people notice. Don't hide out in your church building. Find purposeful ways to be a part of community-wide activities, and shine for Jesus. Instead of competing with events that your community is already planning, get involved in what they are doing and bring Jesus into the mix. Here are a few ideas you can accomplish in a day.

Show You Care. Does your community do a citywide neighborhood cleanup day? Your church should have the largest group there. Wear your church T-shirts and serve joyfully to make an impact.

Marathon Missions. Does your community host an annual marathon, half marathon, or 5K race? Your church can be a valuable sponsor!

➡ Host a water table. Wear your church T-shirts. Smile a lot.

➡ Be an official sponsor (get your church logo on the running shirts).

➡ Put together a care package with an invitation to Sunday worship inside for those who finish the race.

➡ Have church members sign up to run and all wear church T-shirts as they run.

➡ Volunteer church bike riders to be the security team for the runners. They can carry water bottles and a cell phone, in case of an emergency, and ride up and down the path. They can encourage runners and take care of any problems that come up.

➡ Have a big crowd at the finish line, all wearing your church T-shirts, cheering loudly for every runner until the last one crosses the line.

➡ Have a church photographer take photos and pass out cards to view photos on your church website.

||||||||||||||||

Our church decided to get involved in the city's half marathon race. For a few years in a row we sponsored the event. We encouraged as many people in the church as were able to run in the race and everyone else available to serve in other ways. We hosted multiple water tables, played music, and even provided individuals on bicycles as security for the runners. A group of church members cheered at the finish line and congratulated runners as they finished their race. Everyone wore T-shirts with our church name and worked hard to make the event a huge success. The city put our photo in the newspaper and the mayor wrote us a personal letter thanking us for our "beyond the call of duty" attitudes. Making an impact by getting involved in the community's events is always a win!

||||||||||||||||

County Fair Outreach. Get involved in your county fair this year!

➡ Set up a church booth

➡ Plan a phenomenal flash mob

➡ Do free face painting and balloon animals

➡ Volunteer to help collect trash

➡ Get your worship team on the schedule to play live music. Add some creative element, such as a rhythmic sticks team, Scripture-quoting stomp team, choreographed Jesus drill team, or other unique God-focused performance group.

➡ Host a free dinner

➡ Pass out free water bottles

Festival Enthusiast. Find a great way to fully participate in your community's largest festival. Design a memorable booth staffed with joyful volunteers wearing church T-shirts.

➡ Host a walk-through misting booth with a sign that reads, "Worship at [our church] is even more refreshing than this! See you Sunday!" Inexpensive and appreciated on a hot day.

➡ Set up a baby-changing booth with a sign that reads, "Jesus loves the little children, and so do we! See you Sunday at [our church]!"Consider posting photos of your fabulous nursery.

➡ Create a unique booth, like "Free prayer," "How to become a Christian," "How to Go to Heaven," or "Free Prayer Lessons." Be creative and classy with booth design. You'll be surprised at the response.

➡ Tattoo Parlor. Apply temporary cross tattoos or face paint for children.

➡ Serve five-cent bags of popcorn in popcorn bags with church info. Include a creative booth sign that says something like, "Pop on over to [our church] next Sunday!"

➡ Distribute hundreds of helium balloons, foam hats, or plastic fans, imprinted with your church logo.

→ Pull wagons full of iced water, carry a "free water" sign, and pass out bottled water and church brochures.

→ Distribute packets of flower seeds with this question: "If God can make flowers out of seeds, just imagine what He could do with you!"

→ Wear well-designed signboards advertising an upcoming event at your church.

Invisible People. Prepare a homemade dinner for traveling carnival workers at your county fair. And as you minister to others, always share Jesus.

|||||||||||||||

At a citywide event in our town we had a booth for our church. To make it interactive, we printed scavenger hunt cards. We gave every person that stopped at our booth a card and instructed them to watch for our wandering costumed characters (a ninja, a book character, and a cartoon character) and get them to stamp their card. Once they found two, they could bring the card back for a prize. It was a fun scavenger hunt, and brought people to our booth twice, so we had double opportunity to share the gospel with them and invite them to church.

|||||||||||||||

Church Float. Build an awesome float to enter in your town's biggest parade of the year. Go all out in your decor creating a themed float that correlates with the theme of the parade and points all those viewers to God.

→ Each year's float must be first-class and memorable.

→ Recruit the most creative, energetic people in your church to plan big and have a blast representing Jesus in your town.

→ Involve welders, architects, painters, and other specialized people from your church.

→ For example, for the Christmas parade, build a high, fabulous nativity with a live baby. All the extra characters—kings, shepherds, angels, plus costumed snowmen, Santa, and reindeer walk or skate alongside the float, passing out candies and fliers and pointing to the baby. Each time an angel's trumpet sounds, they dramatically bow down toward the Savior.

GET → GOING!

These are just examples. Take a hard look at your own community's events and find ways to be on mission there.

→ Recruit a great choreographer and form a group to walk band style in the parade, stopping often to perform a very brief, perfectly rehearsed rhythmic choreography. Be creative to fit the parade theme and also point the viewers to Jesus. Watch You Tube videos of brief-case brigades, stomp teams, moms with strollers, Bible band, sticks, lawn chair routines, crosses, and more. The routine is similar to a drill team, often tongue in cheek, serious, spellbinding, and absolutely purposeful. The team rehearses the short choreography to absolute perfection, and participates in the parade for a fun entry.

→ Add walkers and a great church sign, such as, "Jesus loves the little children. So does [our church]!"

FOR YOUR NATION AND THE WORLD

Yes, you're far away, but here are a few ways your church or small group can assist with missions for the nation or the world in about a day.

Project for Missions Team. If your church is sending a missions team across the nation or the world, commit a day to do a project to help them. The key is to gather a lot of people and have fun as you serve.

For example, engage your small group to make witnessing bracelets or put together supplies. Or collect small items the ministry team can give their hosts or those they'll minister to. For example, small candies for children, travel-size lotions for women, or a nice gift for the host. If they are ministering in an orphanage, prepare small, easily transportable gifts for each child.

"Encourage the Nations" Day. Collect a list of international missionaries serving all over the world. Gather decor items, snacks, and photos from their countries and have stations set up around the church gym or fellowship hall distinct for each nation. At each station, have plenty of cards, envelopes, and pens. Instruct attendees to try international snacks, enjoy photos, and, most importantly, pray for the missionaries at these places. Have a host at each station to answer questions about the country and to instruct people how to specifically pray for that nation and the missionaries who serve there. Before they leave that station, have each person pick a missionary and write them an encouragement note with a scripture saying, "I prayed for you today." The church can then mail all of the letters to the missionaries.

Cross the Border. Live in a town close to a border? Take a one day missions trip to Canada or Mexico! Gather a team and connect with a local church in that country. Plan ahead to take materials for a project, supplies for an orphanage, or games for a kid's day in the park. As you go, blitz an area sharing the gospel, serving the community, and investing in that local church. Before you leave for the day, take time to worship and pray together with members of the local church community and to encourage them in their ministry.

GET → GOING! Even if you can't go overseas, you can help and encourage a vocational missionary there.

93

On Mission on Vacation. Print a handout for the entire church in early May, challenging them to be intentionally on mission wherever they go on vacation. Help them to connect with a missionary that your denomination supports in the area. Suggest evangelistic/missions projects. Set up an area in the church foyer for people to post the bulletin from a church their family visited while on vacation or on business trips this summer and see how many you can collect.

One-Day Planter Assistance. Talk with a church planter your church supports. Whether the church plant is nearby or across the country, make a plan for a way your small group could do a one-day project to help. For example, print and mail a postcard the church planter has designed.

FOR CHURCH OUTREACH EVENTS
IIIIIIIIIIIIIIIIIIIIIIIIIIIIIIIIIIIIIIIIIIIIIIIIIIII

Tents Everywhere. Plan a father and kids' campout on the church lawn. Invite every child who's attended a church event (VBS, sports, midweek groups, etc.). This is a great ministry within your church, but it becomes missions when church members intentionally invite unchurched friends and include guests who come.

Vendor Extender. Make a list of every business or vendor that your church uses. Include insurance agencies, delivery and postal carriers, painters, printers, repairmen, and so on. Plan a vendor appreciation event. Make it simple and personal. For example, order pizzas, serve smoothies, and give each service provider a small gift as a token of appreciation for their work for your church. Relax and enjoy visiting with them, and show God's love.

The Great Giveaway. Host a monstrous garage sale as a missions project on the church parking lot. The twist: each guest can take any ten items for free. Church members bring lots of great stuff they don't need, so the sale is overflowing with nice items—furniture, bikes, clothes, treasures, and maybe even an old car. Give the items joyfully. When people ask why it's all free tell them about the free gift you have received from God and invite them to know Him. Bonus ideas:

➡ Free lemonade, served joyfully by children
➡ At checkout, present each family with a free Bible or New Testament.
➡ A free video about Jesus
➡ No donation box or sales of any kind
➡ Youth band plays live music at the side on a stage
➡ A bubble station for children
➡ Friendly members are assigned specific hours to converse with shoppers, inviting them for worship on Sunday.
➡ Everything is joyfully given away.

Of course, the real "great giveaway" is Jesus' gift of salvation!

Bring the Guys. Organize a monthly skeet shooting, golfing, fantasy football draft, or video game group. View this as a fun fellowship and huge missions opportunity. Have the men in your church invite their co-workers and lost neighbors to participate.

Flag Football. Start a flag football league for high schoolers as outreach. Each team is required to have three non-church members on their team.

Free Drive-Through Cocoa. On a beautiful cool fall day, set up an attractive sign and well-marked drive-through in your parking lot. Give each person a steaming hot cup of cocoa, with marshmallows, and a printed invitation to Sunday worship.

Summer Adventure Days. Plan day trip adventures for moms and kids. Have moms invite their friends who are not involved in church to your church's day at the zoo, park, children's museum, or craft day sponsored by a local library or fast food restaurant. Befriend guests and share Jesus.

Host a Dog Party. Invite local pet stores to participate by providing goodie bags for dogs, coupons for grooming, or pet supplies, and free pet checkups by a local vet. Have a dog parade around the parking lot and have a "Top Dog" contest where any dog can compete for title of best trick, cutest walk, biggest/smallest dog, most energetic, coolest dog, etc. Give out little trophies and great prizes donated by local pet bakeries, shops, and grooming salons. Have people snacks and dog snacks like peanut butter or ice cream cones.

Open Tournament. Host a volleyball or three-on-three basketball tournament in your church gym or on the lawn. Some could be geared toward young professionals, high schoolers, over 50, and so on.

➡ Have teams from the community and church sign up ahead of time, and encourage church members to invite their unchurched friends to be on their team.
➡ Advertise on a sign outside the church to invite others in the community to sign up.
➡ Create brackets and schedule a full day with back-to-back games.
➡ Have church members sign up to be on cheering squads.
➡ Pass out snacks and drinks.
➡ Share a two-minute devotional with teams before or after they play, and invite them to church on Sunday.
➡ Help with child care throughout the day.
➡ Have a big trophy to give to the winning team and random prizes for participants throughout the day.

Healthy Saturday. Recruit all the doctors, nurses, dentists, and other medical professionals from local churches in your area to provide a free one-day health clinic to your community. Provide general checkups for families with no health care. Encourage all the doctors to pray with patients before they leave or provide a team of church members to conduct an initial interview with each patient complete with information about your church's ministries and a gospel presentation.

GET → GOING!

If God leads you to plan a one-day outreach event, appoint an enthusiastic planning team and get going!

Sports Clinic as Mission. Invite the friendly local high school or college coach to participate and have Christian high school athletes from your church help teach younger children basic skills. Prepare a calendar of your church's summer activities for their age group, and give them to every church member for outreach. Print it on brightly colored paper, and attach a magnet for refrigerator hanging. Include ongoing events— Bible class, choir, Sunday worship service, drama team, church library hours, open gym times and so on. Don't forget Vacation Bible School, camps, all-church picnic, family or youth missions trip, and church sports teams. Consider adding a family skate night, bowling party, Olympic celebration, or art day this summer. Include the church website and contact information.

Fishing Lessons. Have a pond near your house or church? Gather the men from your congregation and have a "free fishing lessons" day. Provide fishing poles, bait, and nets. Invite the community to come out and fish together—and give free lessons to kids who have never fished before. Remember, a lot of these kids probably don't have a father figure in their lives. Now is the chance for men in the church to be fathers to the fatherless (Psalm 68:5).

Mega-Prayerwalk. Map your town and assign specific locations to every church member to prayerwalk the entire town in one day. Keep your eyes open as you go and be prepared to stop and talk with people you pass along the way. Be a light!

FOR YOUR OWN NEIGHBORHOOD
IIIIIIIIIIIIIIIIIIIIIIIIIIIIIIIIIIIIIIIIIIIIIII

Open your own front door and look out. This is where you begin missions. Try some of these one-day ideas.

Unpack Friendship. New neighbors? Go lend a hand. It's stressful enough moving into a new home. Imagine how much of a blessing it would be if someone stopped to help you for a while. Be sure to take an invitation to your church.

Every Neighborhood Cookout. Encourage church members to host a simultaneous neighborhood cookout at their home or apartment this summer. Email or hand deliver an invitation to each neighbor's home. Ask them to bring something to grill, a side dish to share, and a lawn chair. Create a relaxed, fun atmosphere with great Christian music and some toys for kids. Use name tags, and enjoy getting to know each neighbor who comes. Whether it's a small or large group, relax and have a great time with them. In your conversation, invite each individual to your church if they don't attend one.

Craft Night. Host a holiday craft party in your home. Invite all of your co-workers, your kid's friend's moms or your garden club. Be intentional to share about the God who created everything (Colossians 1:16) with them as you create something great together.

Leaf Attack. How many rakes and trash bags can you gather? Get a group of families together and attack a whole neighborhood on a fall day. In one single day, rake as many full yards as you possibly can in one neighborhood. This might be a good ministry in the church neighborhood or a neighborhood that houses many senior adults.

Be sure you knock on the door and ask permission to rake, and give each neighbor an invitation to your church. Imagine the visibility of a whole neighborhood's leaves raked all at once in the middle of the fall! As you rake each yard, pray for the family that lives there. (Be sure to bag the leaves and set them aside for trash pickup.)

Rocking Neighbors. Have a senior adult neighbor? Make some sandwiches and take lunch to their home. Plan on staying for a few hours just to chat and invest in them. Talk about their relationship with God. While you're there, keep an eye out for ways you can serve them. Can you send your teenage son over to change light bulbs? Or your daughter to clean their windows? Do they need a ride to the doctor's office or just someone to check on them once a week? Watch for ways your family can serve them.

Neighborhood Easter Egg Hunt. Challenge church members to host an egg hunt for their own neighbors, and invite them to Sunday worship. Provide printed instructions about organization and being a witness. This is one of our family's favorite outreach events for our neighbors! Be sure your children's Sunday School is ready for new guests on Sunday.

Neighborhood Independence Day Party. Send out invitations early and ask all of your neighbors to come to your home on July 4. Instruct them to bring food and fireworks. Be prepared with outdoor games, a grill for hot dogs, and fireworks of your own to add to the fun. Just as it gets dusk, gather everyone together to thank them for coming. Be sure to let them all know that you love Jesus and are always available if anyone needs anything or wants to talk about God. Give out invitations to your church or to your Sunday school class and let them know they are welcome anytime.

FOR THE HOLIDAYS
||||||||||||||||||||||||||||||||

Holidays bring many missions opportunities, if you'll just be on the ready. Try some of these one-day missions ideas.

New Year's Day Prayer Room. Set up a 24-hour prayer room in your church beginning December 31 and ending January 1 at 12:01 a.m. Invite church members and small groups to sign up for an hour time slot to join together to pray for the lost in your city.

Father's Day Donuts. What does your church already do for Father's Day? Find a way to incorporate the whole community in that celebration. Instead of doing a Donuts for Dad for your church members, make it an outdoor community event. Set up tables of donuts on the front lawn of your church, and invite the whole neighborhood to come for a free breakfast and bring their dad. Have plenty of church members mingling around the tables connecting with dads of all ages.

Free Christmas Cookies or Valentine Cookies. Organize church members to bake cookies, and place in a box or bag along with an invitation to worship, a Bible study, and a church brochure. Create an outdoor sign and drive-through area to joyfully distribute the cookies to community members. If 20 members bake six-dozen cookies each, you could give cookies to 60 families in the community! Remember, this is an outreach, not a cookie exchange.

Mother's Day Photos. Advertise free family photos before and after church on Mother's Day. Make an attractive announcement on social media so church members can forward the invitation to their unchurched friends. Give each family a card inviting them to come back next Sunday for a free printed copy of their photo.

Community Easter Egg Hunt. This can be one of your church's largest, most effective missions plans. This isn't just for church kids! Invite the entire community, and challenge church members to bring lots of unchurched families with children to the event. Small groups can collect eggs and plan nice prize eggs. Train children in your church to meet guests and invite them to their Sunday School next Sunday. Organize well, and before awarding prizes, briefly and creatively tell the Easter story, using puppets, eggs, or kid-friendly drama. Invite everyone to return for worship on Sunday.

National Day of Prayer. Post a sign on the church lawn to welcome passersby to come inside the sanctuary for a few minutes of personal prayer. Create an atmosphere for prayer and have church members sign up for one-hour time slots throughout the day to be there to pray as well and speak with people from the community who come in. At the entrance, provide a prayer guide, with instructions about how to pray, for those who haven't prayed before.

Independence Day Bike Parade. Host a huge citywide Independence Day bicycle parade in your church parking lot. Invite kids in the community to decorate their bike, skateboard, tricycle, hot wheel car, etc., and participate in the parade. Have your pastor ride on a golf cart or ATV to lead the parade. The youth group can walk around giving invitations to church to every family as the parade rolls on.

Fall Festival Upgrade. Whether it's a pumpkin patch or fall festival, a fabulous hayride or trunk-or-treat, a candy-walk or the town's largest-ever-citywide-costumed hokey pokey, do your church's regular fall kids' event, but add a new focus on outreach with these easy tips:

➡ Encourage every church family to bring unchurched friends with them.

➡ Gather family contact information with a ten-second registration card at the entry. Have a follow-up team e-mail each family within 48 hours to thank them for coming and invite them to church.

→ Offer family photos. Tell each family that their photo will be printed and ready for them to pick up in the church foyer on Sunday.

→ Purchase candy and toys that say something about Jesus on them to give away as prizes.

→ Give every family a card with all church children's events listed.

→ Have a "Meet the Pastor" booth near the entrance so your pastor can connect easily with families.

→ Require every children's worker to be present and give them instruction on how to engage children and families that are new and invite them to their class.

||||||||||||||||

The single adults' class in our church designed a gorgeous photo area for our church's fall festival. They recruited photographers, set up tripods, and snapped a posed photo of each child. (Be sure you have a photo release form for parents to sign ahead of time.) Parents received a card inviting them to pick up their child's photo in the church foyer on Sunday. How missional!

||||||||||||||||

Pumpkin Decorating Competition. Display an invitation banner and gobs of pumpkins outside. Attenders pick a pumpkin, decorate it, and enter their creation into the contest. Provide decorating supplies and carving utensils. Have anonymous judges vote for the winners in each category and give out prizes. Before you announce the winners, share the gospel with the group, and invite them to worship on Sunday. Contestants take home their pumpkins along with an invitation to church.

Halloween Outreach. Is there an area of town where all the kids go for trick or treating? Set up a tent in an open field or a park there and do an outreach on Halloween night.

→ Have lots of candy to hand out.

→ Give an invitation to your next children's event to every child.

→ Put together a drama team to perform. They can draw a crowd and then share the gospel.

→ Be ready to pray with people as God gives you opportunity.

Thanksgiving Turkey Smoking Campout. Invite anyone in the community to join your church's men's group for an all-night turkey-smoking event the evening before Thanksgiving. Each person brings their own turkey to smoke and can also bring lawn chairs, a tent, sleeping bag, etc. While everyone enjoys spending time together and preparing their Thanksgiving meals, have your church members guide conversations toward all God has done in their families and how men can lead their families to be thankful in light of Thanksgiving.

Feast Ingredients. Collect all the ingredients for a fabulous Thanksgiving dinner—from the turkey to pie fixings—and deliver them to needy families. Pray with them when you deliver the food, giving thanks to God.

> *I have not kept the good news of your justice hidden in my heart; I have talked about your faithfulness and saving power. I have told everyone in the great assembly of your unfailing love and faithfulness.* —Psalm 40:10

Serve Thanksgiving Dinner. Consider organizing Thanksgiving dinner for the needy.

Morph Merry into Missions. In November, print an attractive list of all your church's December events, particularly those that would be of interest to non-Christians. Just list the date, event name, and church website for more info, and "You're invited!" Ask all church members to give the list to friends and neighbors who may not know Jesus.

Christmas Cookies. Have a Christmas cookie decorating day at your home for all of your neighbors. Have sugar cookies ready for people to decorate. Don't forget to share the real reason for the Christmas season.

Community Christmas Program. Does your church choir put on a Christmas program? Instead of doing it in your church, rent out a local theater and perform there. Open it up to the whole community, and be sure to share the gospel boldly from the stage.

Pack and Pray. Pack and deliver boxes of Christmas dinner food or ingredients to people in need on Christmas Day. This could be a great project for a group of people from your church who don't have family in town that day.

Live Nativity Scene. Assign church members to mingle, provide free hot chocolate, and be prepared to jump in wherever needed. Got a farmer in your church who will loan out some animals? Live animals are always a hit. Make it into an enormous outreach to the community.

➡ Create a fabulous stable with costumes and props.
➡ Advertise well ahead, using social media, so families can register; adults and kids can participate in ten-minute shifts as nativity characters.
➡ Schedule a large group of volunteers to rotate participants through "The Real Christmas Story," provide instructions, help with costuming, and wrangle any live nativity animals.
➡ Have church members intermingled with guests and invite each person to Sunday School.

One-by-One Nativity. Find a nativity scene with multiple pieces. Choose a neighbor, co-worker, family, or individual you know and plan ahead to deliver the nativity to them one piece at a time for the month of December. Get creative in secretly delivering the pieces to the doorstep, at their work or school, through a neighbor, etc. Begin with the empty stable, and slowly fill up the stable with all of the pieces—each piece accompanied with an encouraging note for the family. Save baby Jesus for last, and deliver Him in person on Christmas morning! It's Christmas, so don't stay long. But take time to pray with them, tell them how much their friendship means to you and also tell them how much Jesus means to you as the real meaning of Christmas.

Christmas Tea. Challenge church members to host a neighborhood Christmas Tea. Help them develop invitations, a relaxed program, and name tags. Print a list of Christmas events and worship services to give each guest.

Cookie Christmas Party. Make your small group's Christmas party evangelistic! Instead of an evening of dining and gifts for each other, consider making this year's Christmas party an all-day event. On a Saturday in December, make plans to meet all day to bake and decorate cookies together. Make as many as you can and package them in ziplock bags. Prepare invitations to your church, and attach them to each bag of cookies. Then, go out to your neighborhood! Deliver the bags of cookies door to door as you sing Christmas carols. End the night praying together for God's blessing over every invitation and gift you handed out.

GET GOING!

Any holiday can provide an opportunity to share about Jesus. Plan ahead. Be creative. Be on mission.

chapter 4

ONE-WEEK MISSIONS IDEAS

R eady to step it up a notch? Grow your one-day missions project into a five to seven day missions trip. Gather a team and invest a week of your life in a fruitful missions project or missions trip.

FOR THE COMMUNITY

You don't even have to leave home to do missions. These one-week projects can accomplish missions right in your own town.

Dinner Theater Evangelism. Plan a quality annual summer dinner theater with a full-length evangelistic Christian drama and steak dinner. A church member who taught theater in the local high school directed ours each summer, and it was an evangelistic success! Invite artists to assist with backdrops and carpenters to build sets. Provide half-price tickets and best seats for members who commit to bring lost friends, and get ready to use your "sold out" sign.

||||||||||||||||

For a few summers, our youth group put on a summer dinner theater. It was a major all-hands-on-deck event! A local theater teacher who also ended up becoming a member of our church stepped in to be the director. She chose an evangelistic script (even wrote one of her own the second year), held auditions at the beginning of summer, and had rehearsals and stage, lighting, and sound design workdays all summer long. By the end of the summer, we had an impressive performance prepared with a full set, lighting, sound, and more. Members of the church got on board to create sets and props, serve tables for the dinner, advertise, etc. It was a great community event and, at the end of the performance, we saw multiple people come to know Christ!

||||||||||||||||

Pray for the Unreached. Host a week of prayer for an unreached people group. Get statistics, prayer points, photos, details from missionaries who might be serving there, etc. Open up a room at your church (or your living room) as a 24-hour prayer space, specifically praying for that one nation for a week solid (or a day for a smaller group). Have a sign-up sheet so people can sign up as a family, small group, or individual to come to pray for an hour time slot. Make the prayer interactive with prayer stations. At each station, have instructions written out for what they are to do:

→ Identity in Christ—Set up an area with mirrors all around. On each mirror, write a Scripture that defines your identity in Christ. Pray for unreached people around the world to come to know God as the One who determines their worth and identity.

→ Sticky-note prayers—Find a large map of the world (or draw one) and put it on a wall. Have sticky notes and pens on a table by the map instructing people to write out a one-sentence prayer for a nation of the world, then stick it to the nation. Cover the whole world with prayer.

→ Missionary prayer—Have photos of missionaries your church supports and a few prayer points below each one detailing where they serve and what their needs are. Instruct participants to pray for each one by name.

→ Pray for the lost—Have a pile of glass pebbles (you can get these at any craft store) and some fine-point permanent markers. Set up a small "river" with blue paper, or use a small fountain if you have one. Write the first name of someone in your life who is not a believer on a pebble and place it in the river praying for the fresh water of God to wash them today as you pray for their salvation.

→ Repentance station—Purchase dissolving paper from a craft store. At one station, instruct individuals to write on a slip of paper the sins in their life that they need to ask forgiveness for. Provide a large bowl of water for them to drop the paper into after they pray asking God for cleansing . . . then watch the sin disappear.

→ The net—Get a large flat fishing net and hang it on the wall. Behind the net, put up photos of the nation or people group you are praying for. Use large colorful photos and have a few text pieces that show statistics about the country's needs or current state. As people come to the net to pray, instruct them to pray for the missionaries and churches serving in this nation to be able to draw the net and capture these people's hearts with the message of Christ.

→ Carry the weight—Have a few very large rocks on the floor next to some small pillows. Instruct those praying to kneel on a pillow and hold up one of the rocks at arm's-length in front of them while they pray for the needs of a specific missionary. Feeling the weight of the rock weakening their arms will give them a physical picture of the weight that this ministry has on the missionary serving there. Pray for physical, emotional, and spiritual strength for those sacrificing for the gospel.

Milestone Marking. If your church or the church plant you support has a major milestone, such as purchasing property, a launch of a new service, or the completion of a new building, plan a one-week prayer commitment for your entire church. Make a chart of every hour in the week. People sign up for one particular hour to pray. They can pray at home or at the church in a designated location. Send an e-mail reminder of their prayer hour, with a list of ways to pray.

Missions Stay-Cation. Instead of a stay-cation, plan a one-week missions trip in your community. One week of crazy schedule and eternal investment you will never forget.

➡ Call local hospitals, shelters, and ministries, and set up projects for the week. Gather a team of people from your church, and go to a different place every day serving in the name of Jesus.

➡ Have prayertimes for your city on the highest point in town—a mountain, hilltop, or a parking garage rooftop—get somewhere where you can see the whole city as you pray.

➡ Work with a neighborhood association or the city to clean up a park.

➡ Hang out at bus stops and share the gospel. You'll have a captive audience every 15–20 minutes!

➡ Pass out flyers to an upcoming church event or worship service to every home in the area surrounding your church.

➡ Can't get a week off of work? Plan these events every day for a week from 5:30 to 9 p.m.!

Citywide Thanksgiving Art Exhibit. In early fall, begin to solicit entries from church members, friends, local artists, art clubs, and classes. Using any medium, artists illustrate Thanksgiving-themed Scripture. Schedule a submission deadline for the end of October. Challenge members to ask everyone they know who is an artist; unchurched artists are welcomed and included. Display the art in the church foyer throughout November. Ask entrants to come for worship on one specific Sunday.

Last Week of School Focus. Do you teach a children's class at your church? Have a one-week missions focus for your class, and invite each child's family to participate. Have a small task every day the last week of school that will allow students to be a blessing to their classmates, faculty, and staff at their school. Get together as a class each afternoon for 30 minutes to prepare the blessing for the next day and pray for the people they deliver it to.

→ **Day 1:** Take time after church Sunday to pray for teachers and staff at their school. Write thank you notes and deliver them Monday.

→ **Day 2:** Put together goodie bags for each child to take to school. With permission from their teacher, pass them out to all the kids in a particular class (include prepackaged candies or other small non-edible items). And be sure to include, "I'm praying for you this week," on a note from the student.

→ **Day 3:** Buy some plain white coffee mugs and tons of permanent markers. Have children decorate a mug with "Greatest Principal/ Teacher Ever" to deliver to their teacher or principal.

→ **Day 4:** Organize an age appropriate art project for your group. Have children make projects and deliver them to their school janitors. Be sure to instruct kids to say, "Thank you for serving me all year long."

→ **Day 5:** Make an eye-catching invitation for your church's VBS, children's/youth camp, or fun event happening this summer. Get permission ahead of time to bring enough copies to send an invitation home with every student in your class (or whole school). Before you run the copies, have the student write a personal note of invitation, "I'm going to the game night come with me! —Johnny."

→ **Day 6:** Plan a pool party or day at the park for the whole class to celebrate the last day of school. Challenge every child to bring one friend who does not go to your church with them to the party. Be prepared with church invitations and parents who are ready to connect with visitor's parents, too.

Rethink Vacation Bible School. If your church's VBS is simply a fun camp for your own church kids, you're missing a huge missions opportunity. Yes, it's awesome for church members' children, but it's also an enormous opportunity to teach them to welcome kids who are unchurched. VBS as mission isn't just for missions trips. Do it at home!

→ If your church has a missions team, involve them in this rethink!

→ Establish a publicity plan, including exterior signs and social media.

→ Provide commitment cards for church members to commit to invite, transport, or serve in this year's VBS.

→ Help all church members (even those with no children!) become involved in inviting unchurched neighbors and acquaintances' children.

→ Involve children in your church as missionaries to invite their friends who don't go to church to come with them to VBS. Provide helium balloons with invitations tied to them, and ask kids to deliver a balloon invitation to a friend(s).

→ Order fun car flags with your church logo on them for every church member who will commit to invite and transport unchurched friends and neighbors to VBS.

→ Print invitation cards for members to deliver to neighbors. If VBS is near the first of summer, children can take cards to their friends before school lets out.

→ Form a team to personally contact and register every child who attended anything at your church last year—Sunday School guests, sports, fall festival, day care, missions or midweek groups, inactive Sunday School members. Don't skip this step!

→ If parents of guests want to help, welcome them. Pair them with another church member to serve snacks or help in another way.

→ Provide "free transportation" invitations for church members to give each child in their neighborhood. Some may even have to make two trips!

➡ Intentionally invite children in need. Deliver invitations to nearby apartment complexes. Seek out refugees, immigrants, children in the neediest parts of the community, and make a plan for transportation and full involvement.

➡ Train teachers to be aware of unchurched guests and to treasure each one. Allow them to participate just as much as members, and don't expect them to know Bible stories if they haven't been to church before.

➡ Train every teacher (and teens who teach) how to explain God's plan of salvation to children, and how to share conversationally about how God impacts their daily life. Evangelism must be a priority, not an afterthought.

➡ Form a prayer team to lift up those children in prayer daily.

➡ Make a detailed follow-up plan for families of VBS guests. Follow up by phone or e-mail the Saturday after VBS, and invite each family to worship that Sunday. Plan a date the week after VBS for personal visits to homes of unchurched children, and put that date on the VBS workers' schedule as part of their ministry responsibilities. Be sure to include all members who work in weekly children's ministry, such as Sunday School, missions, or midweek groups, choirs, or sports. Their presence on outreach visits is greatly beneficial. This is as important as all your other planning.

➡ Provide a contact list of guests who attended VBS to every children's Sunday School department worker.

➡ For the VBS offering, all those pennies add up, and children learn to love missions. Consider a missions need in your own community, or a missions project with a missionary your church supports, and let the children know the money will be designated specifically for that mission.

➡ On the last day of VBS, send a note home with each unchurched guest inviting their parents to a brunch before next Sunday's worship. At the brunch, the pastor can converse with parents, answer their questions about the church, share God's plan of salvation, and encourage them to bring the family to worship.

▐▐▐▐▐▐▐▐▐▐▐▐▐▐

There, on the lawn of our historic church, stood a 30-foot-tall gorilla balloon holding a huge invitation to Vacation Bible School. It was a hilarious spectacle. We had a record number of unchurched children who attended that year, and several families came to know God . . . because of a gorilla. Outdoor advertising says, "Come on in!"

▐▐▐▐▐▐▐▐▐▐▐▐▐▐

Extended VBS. Plan an arts program for kids on the afternoons of Vacation Bible School, with a focus on God, using a variety of mediums. This creative extension of VBS may enable some additional children to attend.

Senior Care Facility VBS. Host a one-week Vacation Bible School for senior adults in a local senior care facility. Plan music, crafts, Bible stories, and recreation, all configured for senior adults. Have fun, show God's love, and clearly explain God's plan of salvation. Or plan one for the local senior center. Many are looking for classes or activities for senior adults. Make it a week that will impact eternity.

Off-Site Vacation Bible School. Where are pockets of children in your town who couldn't otherwise attend a Vacation Bible School? Take it to them! An apartment complex? A migrant community? A children's group home? A mobile home park? A homeless community? Could you host a VBS in a park near where many immigrants reside? Work with the correct authorities to plan VBS in an outdoor area or a community center.

Backyard Bible Club. Talk with your church leaders about bringing VBS to the street—your street!

Backyards Everywhere. Even better, plan simultaneous VBS events in yards across the city. Chart a huge map of locations, and invite the community to come.

|||||||||||||||

There was a VBS sign in front of our house and a canopy tent in the backyard. All the neighborhood children came and brought friends. We personally delivered invitations to every neighbor with children and asked them to bring friends. Plenty of teen and adult volunteers shared the planning and teaching. The music was fabulous, the play was noisy and hilarious, and many children were entranced with the story of Jesus for the first time. Most importantly, we were able to continue the ministry to these neighbors long term—because we lived by them!

|||||||||||||||

Kids Music Camp. Host a children's music camp week at the church as an outreach. Ask every child in your church to bring at least one unchurched friend, and sing lots of great Christian music. It could be a musical or fun worship songs. Be sure that starring roles aren't exclusively for members. On the following Sunday, let the campers sing a song during worship, or use those choruses as the worship music, with children mixed with the choir or praise team.

Kids Art Camp. Plan an art camp for your community.

→ Charge a small registration fee to help cover the cost of supplies.

→ Assign artists in the church to teach a variety of art mediums— music, mime, photography, sculpture, puppetry, watercolor, videography, clowning, woodcarving, murals, quilting, graphic art, decorating, stained glass, costume design, metalwork, needle point, media arts, poetry—all focused on God's creation.

→ Talk with your city library about displaying some of the artwork at the end of the week.

→ Have an art Sunday at the end of the week. Ask your pastor to preach a message about the creativity of God and artwork can be displayed around the room.

██████████████

When I lived in England, a missions team from Texas came a few years in a row to do an art camp with the youth in our city. We began by taking art out to the skate park where kids hung out and inviting them to join in on the group projects. We then invited them to the church for the rest of the week to participate in a free art camp every day from 12 to 3 p.m. We had different projects each day, self-portraits, graffiti art, sculptures, face-molds, etc. that all pointed back to a Scripture and a casual "God talk." This harsh group of teenagers was able to use art to put words to their emotions and fears. That led to tons of salvations over the years.

██████████████

Decorate to Evangelize. If your church is blessed with a gym and you encourage nonmembers to use it, plan a week-long decorating project to embellish its decor and create a stationary witness for those who come. Work with a decorator and a graphic artist to create an excellent plan with a beautiful color scheme and God-focused decor. Schedule specific hours for volunteer painters, cleaners, carpenters, and so on.

→ Use a vinyl-cutting machine to print wall Scripture. Carefully select font and size. Encourage church members to put the Scriptures in their home, school classrooms, or workplaces and watch for opportunities to talk about the Scripture with others. Art can point to God, even in the exercise room. All wall art should be selected as an inspirational witness.

→ Use contemporary graphic banners with athletic-themed Scriptures high on gym walls. Example, "Be strong in the Lord. —Ephesians 6:10"

→ If you have a walking track, share God's plan of salvation to read as they walk. For example, "Step one. Recognize that you are a sinner. The Bible says that all have sinned and come short of God's glory. Romans 3:23"

➡ Be sure there are witnessing tracts on display. Consider using technology like a slide presentation on the computer.

➡ Advertise upcoming church events prominently, tastefully, and enthusiastically.

➡ See ideas for welcoming nonmembers to your gym in Chapter 5.

Prisoner Christmas Project. Work with the chaplain to provide Christmas cards for each prisoner. Encourage the prisoner to write a sincere personal letter to family and friends. Often that will be the only gift they can give. If possible, provide stamps as well.

Hallelujah Handbags. If there is a women's prison nearby, work with a chaplain there to do this awesome project we learned about from the Rankin County, Mississippi, Christian Women's Job Corps® website, Rankincwjc.org: First, collect large, new or gently used handbags. Next, gather carefully selected items that a woman leaving prison might need immediately. For example, snacks, lotion, wallet, gift card to the local grocery store, hairbrush, makeup starter set, etc. Write a personal note from your church to promise your prayers and invite her to worship. Provide these nice bags to the chaplain as often as needed.

Host a Missions Conference. One fantastic way to involve your entire church in missions is to hold a missions conference at your church.

➡ Invite all of the ministries, church planters, and missionaries that your church directly supports to set up a booth and have a large area where people in your church can visit with them to learn about their ministries.

➡ Plan a worship service and have a dynamic missionary or church planter as your keynote speaker to challenge and encourage your church to be on mission.

→ Have corporate times of prayer to lift up each ministry or pray for other potential ministry opportunities in cities or nations, near and far.

→ Hold breakout sessions, and ask each of the church planters or missionaries to share about their ministry and how individuals in your church can be involved.

→ Plan missions trips to each of your partners all year long and have the dates finalized in time for the missions conference so you can announce them. Encourage every person to be involved in at least one missions trip or project with one of your partners.

→ Host a dinner and have a ministry partner at each table to engage in conversation with your church members.

→ Instead of having the guests sleep in a local hotel, recruit loving homes in your church to host a missionary for the weekend providing meals, a place to sleep, and engaging conversation. Strategically ask people who might be leading a missions team or serving on a missions team to that missionary's area this year.

→ At the end of the weekend, hold a time of commitment. Invite church members to indicate on a commitment card their family's intent to sign up for a certain missions trip or to pray for a specific ministry this year. Have a visible way for them to "hand in" their commitment card and make their commitment to the church and to the missionaries.

||||||||||||||||

One of our partner churches holds a missions conference every year. For weeks ahead of time, they ask families to pray about how much they would give above and beyond their tithe to this specific missions offering. They then take up their church's missions offering and commitment cards during one specific offering time. As a church planter who is supported by this church, it was an incredibly humbling and encouraging moment to see the entire church filing down to the altar to place their card or their offering on the steps at the front of the sanctuary one after the next. The best part was how excited the people were! They laughed and clapped and celebrate—excited that God had provided for them to provide for us! What a picture of the church being the church.

IIIIIIIIIIIII

Assess the Address. This week-long leadership project helps your church or small group leadership or missions team determine where to begin on mission. Take a close look, statistically, at the "missions field" around your church.

➡ Make daily assignments, and meet for a half hour each day to report your findings.

➡ Set up a small room for this project. Post a paper map on a wall, and cover the walls of your meeting room with paper. As you meet and brainstorm, write every missions idea on the walls.

➡ Use the Community Questionnaire in the appendix for assignments and discussion topics for potential missions ideas. Different leaders are assigned to gather the various statistics and community information before the next day's meeting and discussion.

➡ Carefully consider the unique qualities of your church's location. Make a list. Consider how God can use that location to help you be on mission for Him, then proactively do it. Some examples:

  • A church in the airport flight path could paint huge letters on their flat roof proclaiming, "God loves you!"

  • A church on the parade route could plan an outreach during parades.

  • A church on a river could do outdoor baptisms and invite the neighbors.

  • A church in a neighborhood could target specific blocks for an ongoing missions project.

  • A church in the vicinity of the community's festivals can open the church as a ministry (not a fundraiser). Serve cobbler or cold water. Or present great live music and a shade, and let people use the restrooms.

- If your location and building is historical, offer free tours.
- If your church is on a race route, set up your own great water table or cheering squad.
- If your church is next to a cancer-treatment facility, provide housing and a car for families to drive, or a prayer room.
- If your church is on the beach or near a ski lodge or campground, offer a special evangelistic Bible class or worship service for tourists there.

➜ Carefully consider the varieties of lostness. Use a marker to section off the county or city map, and assign each leader one area to drive, observe, and pray before your missions findings meeting.

➜ Brainstorm needs and potential missions projects in your community, writing every idea—good or bad, cheap or expensive, reasonable or not—on the walls of your meeting room.

After your week of observation, research, and prayer, make specific plans to impact those outside your church doors and be on mission for God, beginning now.

GET→GOING! These are just a sampling of ways to be on mission in your community. Ask God to show your church or small group new ways to touch your town for Him.

‖‖‖‖‖‖‖‖‖‖‖‖‖

Afterward, we dubbed it the frozen Christmas carols. Our Houston church staged an awesome drive-through Christmas event for our community. Huge backdrops were built depicting several Christmas carols that relayed the real Christmas story. They were spaced throughout the drive-through route in our parking lot. Piped music played and costumed characters moved as each car drove slowly through the scenes. As a car arrived, they received a brochure explaining the story, a church invitation, and hot cocoa for each person. Rare for Houston, the last day's weather was frigid. Cars were still lined down the road to see the God-story! Our frozen Christmas carols were the talk of the town, and God was honored as our church served the community.

‖‖‖‖‖‖‖‖‖‖‖‖‖

FOR TAKING A MISSIONS TRIP
‖‖‖‖‖‖‖‖‖‖‖‖‖‖‖‖‖‖‖‖‖‖‖‖‖‖‖‖‖‖‖‖‖‖‖‖‖‖

When a church or small group is ready to commit a week or two for missions, they often take a missions trip. Here are a few ideas to get you started:

Family Missions. Turn your family vacation into a missions trip. Gather a few other families from your church or small group and go to your favorite vacation destination together. Before you go, find a local church or church plant in that area to connect with while you are there. Call ahead and ask how you can serve them.

→ Can you bring supplies from your church to donate to them for an outreach event?

→ If you've established a close relationship, you can give the church planter and his wife a much needed date night by offering to watch their kids for an evening or take them with your family to the beach so mom and dad can have a day together.

➡ Plan on being there on a Sunday to worship with their church.

➡ Participate in their Sunday School classes or small groups that week.

➡ Go to lunch with a few people from the congregation just to encourage them after church on Sunday.

➡ Plan to take one full day of your vacation to serve the church by doing some landscaping, taking flyers around town for them, or organizing a youth game night.

➡ Schedule it so that every morning from 9 a.m. to noon you are doing a project with/for the church and then the afternoons and evenings are vacation time for your families.

My ambition has always been to preach the Good News where the name of Christ has never been heard, rather than where a church has already been started by someone else. —Romans 15:20

And the Good News about the Kingdom will be preached throughout the whole world, so that all nations will hear it; and then the end will come. —Matthew 24:14

Missions Trip Projects. The sky is the limit for all the different types of missions trip projects! It's vital that you carefully consult with the missionary or planter about the trip's purpose. You may want to build a building . . . but what the missionary really needs is for you to sit with their people and peel *nopales* (a Mexican fruit). Ask God to give direction and wisdom as you plan.

The next several pages are just a few ideas to get you thinking about purposeful missions trips.

Repair Tractors. Take a group of mechanics from your church to a farming community or country where their equipment is failing. Your expertise and tools can change everything for their businesses and lifestyle, not to mention the effect your gracious representation of Jesus may have for them eternally.

Inner-City Trip. The jungles of Africa need Jesus. So does the major city in the next state! Consider doing a missions trip to an urban city around your area. Offer a kids camp, work with an existing benevolence ministry, go to the hard places within the city, and be the light of Christ there.

Street Outreach. Organize your group around a solid plan to do street outreaches effectively.

➡ Divide the group into four teams: the music team, the worship dance team, the drama team, and the evangelism team.

➡ Head out to a park, courtyard, or open area in the town.

➡ When you arrive, first have the music team set up and start playing. Their job is to draw a crowd.

➡ Once there's a bit of a crowd, the dance team steps up and performs a worshipful, upbeat dance to get the crowd's attention.

➡ Next up is the drama team. Prepare a short drama (it's best if it has no words, just set to music) that is evangelistic in nature.

➡ As soon as the drama is over, have a team member share his or her testimony with the gospel.

➡ As all of this is happening, prepare the evangelism team (and what-ever teams are not currently doing something) to mingle in the crowd talking and praying with people and leading them to Christ.

➡ Be sure you have a local church there as well to help with follow up.

Pass Out Bibles. Have a Bible drive at your church and collect as many new Bibles as you can. If the missions trip is to another country, purchase Bibles in that native language. When you go on your missions trip, pass out Bibles in as many homes as possible. Talk about Jesus.

Include an invitation to join the local church you are working alongside for worship.

||||||||||||||

In Vancouver, we were aghast to learn of the extreme difficulties for churches to purchase property. In Ukraine, we heard a young pastor tell of watching his father, a pastor, shot in the head because of his ministry. When asked if they'd ever stepped inside a church building, not one of several hundred high school students in Germany raised their hand. After a Bible story about Paul, a child in our Texas VBS class asked, "Which one of you is Paul?" America, itself, is one of our world's greatest missions fields. The need for sharing Jesus is enormous, both in your town, your nation, and across your world. Share Jesus.

||||||||||||||

Bible Story Mural. Get permission to take a group of skilled artists into an area of town that needs a face lift. Have the artist draw the mural while others fill it in. Invite passersby to join in the fun and give them a section of the mural to fill in with a specific color. As you paint, share the love of Jesus.

Sewing Machines. A missions trip to a developing country could include teaching locals a skill set and helping them begin their own business. For example, take sewing machines, fabric, and everything needed to start a sewing business. Provide one-on-one sewing lessons and help them get started.

Medical Team. Gather all of the medical professionals in your area and take a trip to a country where basic medical treatment is not available. Have medical students in your church? Include them. Offer free clinics to administer injections, prescribe medication, and perform general checkups for free. Dentists can do the same! Take basic equipment to do checkups and cleanings. Present each person with a new toothbrush, toothpaste, and floss. This would be ideal for a developing country.

||||||||||||||

A team of doctors in our Texas church planned an annual medical missions trip to a different remote town in Mexico. Most towns had never had medical care of any kind. Working with our local missionaries, they would select the site. Preparation took the entire year—sorting medicines, collecting supplies, glasses, and Spanish Bibles, preparing their vehicle with exam, surgery, and dental rooms, and praying together. The team of doctors, dentists, nurses, and other volunteers spent long, hot daylight hours meeting medical needs, while non-medical volunteers took care of entrance interviews, planned activities and Bible teaching for the children, and shared Jesus with every person in line. Evenings were spent in a central area of town preaching, sharing testimonies, visiting with people, and singing about Jesus. The regional missionary would participate and follow up with new Christians afterward.

||||||||||||||

Then He sent them to proclaim the kingdom of God and to heal the sick. —Luke 9:2 (HCSB)

||||||||||||||

For many years, one young boy accompanied his parents, who were not medical professionals, on medical missions trips. He grew up to be a successful doctor who led teams of fellow doctors to continue serving God in rural Mexican towns.

||||||||||||||

Music Minor. If your church does an annual choir missions trip, don't forget the missions! Take your music outside the walls of the church and have half of your team in the crowd sharing with people who come to listen. Include evangelistic projects, and use the music to draw people. If your concert is scheduled at a church, ask permission to make invitation flyers, and take them around the church's neighborhood. Provide refreshments as guests arrive or after the concert so your whole choir can invest in people who come. Be intentional about sharing your personal testimony with as many people as you can during that time.

Music Event. Have live musicians perform a free concert in a city park or neighborhood. As you invite the town for the concert, be prepared to share Jesus with everyone as they hang out and listen. Be certain that songs clearly present the gospel message and are understandable and simple for the hearers. Incorporate monologues, testimonies, or a simple drama to further explain. The focus is on Jesus.

Concert on the Square. Schedule the missions trip during a major festival in the city or country where you'll minister. Book your music group for a stage time at the festival. Share Jesus using a concert, and, if possible, put some of the local church members and the pastor in a visible role. Staff a church booth, too, using ideas from Chapter 3 festival ideas.

||||||||||||||

A small Celtic band comprised half of our missions team to Apolda, Germany. Their unique instruments and Christian music was captivating, and they drew crowds in the mall, street corners, and other public places. Here's what made it an effective mission: the German pastor and some church members were there among the crowd, conversing and inviting listeners to worship at the church where they'd sing on Sunday. The rest of the missions team was among the crowd, too, passing out invitations, striking up conversations, sharing Jesus, and introducing folks to the local pastor.

||||||||||||||

Conduct a Survey. Go to a populated area with clipboards and paper. Ask the missionary/church planter what they think the people in their city would respond to best and do a survey on that topic. You might ask questions such as:

➡ What do you think about when you hear the name Jesus?

➡ What do you think of church?

➡ Do you think God exists?

➡ What do you think God cares about?

As you end the survey with each person ask them if you can tell them what you think about each question as well.

Distribute Flyers. Many missionaries and church plants would be thrilled for a team to come and go door-to-door or around town passing out information flyers for an event or weekly worship service. It seems like a simple job, but when you have a small congregation as a church plant or when you're serving as a missionary with your family, it can be overwhelming to think about canvasing a whole neighborhood. Your team could do this in a single day.

Game Nights. Bring as many board games as you can manage and set up for a family game night for all of the missionary's neighbors or unchurched acquaintances. Display games for all ages on tables around a room or blankets in a park. At each game, have at least one person from your team explain the game, play with those who come, and intentionally share the gospel as they play and invest in people.

||||||||||||||

I still remember the song we sang on the bus headed for a south Texas missions trip. I was just a girl, and was filled with anticipation and excitement to help with a Vacation Bible School in an impoverished region. Include your children in missions.

||||||||||||||

Distribute Eyeglasses. A group of optometrists (or trained volunteers) can distribute eyeglasses to those who can't afford them. Train the team members to give a basic eye exam and fit each person with glasses. Your church can collect discarded prescription glasses to use for the mission.

Street Evangelism. Get bold and go out on the street to talk with people about Jesus. This works especially well when you travel to another country, as it is easy to start up a conversation with someone curious about your accent. Be bold in sharing the gospel and always end by saying, "Is that something you would like to have today?"

Sports Camp. Sports always draw a crowd. Host a free sports camp in a local park for kids or teens. Give basic lessons and teach about good sportsmanship. Always take time to do a Bible lesson and teach participants (in an age-appropriate way) how the Bible gives us instruction in activities like sports and trains us how to play with excellence and joy.

|||||||||||||||

My son went on a missions trip to Israel to help lead a basketball camp. Their team of coaches actually had the opportunity to scrimmage with the Palestinian Olympic team! You never know what doors God may open when you're on mission. Be ready.

|||||||||||||||

Bicycle Missions Trip. Work with your denominational missionaries in a city or country where bicycling is a primary form of transportation. Bike across the city or area, stopping to spend a few days with missionaries or churches along the way, with specific projects to help them. A key goal is to meet other local cyclists, get to know each other, and share Jesus.

Teach English. On an overseas missions trip, get permission to go into a local school and teach in their English class. One simple teaching method is to use American holidays to teach American culture and language. Have each person on your team bring photos from family holidays to give students a visual. Christmas and Easter are good to use, but the most fun will be Thanksgiving (only a few other countries have this holiday, so it's always interesting). Have them make turkey hands, Pilgrim hats, and Native American headdresses. Use the opportunity to talk about being thankful to God for all He has provided.

Go Door-to-Door. Classic, but still powerful! Teach your team how to start the conversation about Jesus. Don't be pushy. As each person answers the door, introduce yourself and ask if they would be interested in hearing about Jesus. Have a Bible to present to each home and invite them to the local church you are ministering alongside.

||||||||||||||||

Our missions trip to Wiesbaden, Germany, was primarily to teach personal evangelism in an English-speaking church near the American military base. As God's timing would have it, Operation Desert Storm was launched nearby. The base was on lock down. There were daily bomb drills in the school, and troops were being deployed to the war zone. Many troops were asking colleagues questions about heaven and death. One church member, who was a military doctor, wanted to share Jesus with a co-worker. As we sat in his living room, that co-worker joyfully prayed to accept God's gift of salvation! "I knew you were a Christian," he told the doctor, "but I couldn't get up the courage to ask you about it." Many around us are dying to know Jesus. Don't be afraid to introduce Him.

||||||||||||||||

Pray a Lot. Every chance you get on a trip, stop and pray. Have a few times on your trip where your team gathers to pray for an hour or two. Invite the missionary or members of the local church to join you and take time to pray specifically over each of them as they live and serve in their city. Don't neglect the power of prayer to change a nation!

REMEMBER:

When planning a missions trip, ask the missionary or church planter exactly what type of ministry would help open evangelistic doors for their church.

Vacation Bible School. Many churches already do a VBS or kids camp week at their own church. Offer to take your VBS on the road this year! After your church's event, you can take the decorations, supplies, Bible study materials, music, etc., along with a team of people who have already taught the lessons for the week and reproduce it again somewhere else. This makes for minimal team training (because they're already doing it at your church first). Plan activities for parents who may stay during VBS.

Orphanage Outreach. Playing with kids in an orphanage is simple, yet profound. Kids have a great love language . . . and it is "play." Simply hanging out and playing with children in an orphanage can be an incredible outreach as you show them the love and attention of Christ through your actions. Get permission from the orphanage to share stories about Jesus as you play.

Shield a Badge with Prayer. Assign a different church member a police officer in your town to pray for—until every police officer has a church member praying for him or her. Send occasional notes to remind them of your prayers and deliver a tangible reminder of your church's prayers to the precinct office. Examples: a plaque with a prayer promise and Scripture or a set of coffee mugs with Scripture and your church's name.

||||||||||||||

When our church members committed to pray for an individual policeman in our town for a year, the police department hung our Scripture plaque above their entry door. A few members even received letters of gratitude from their police officer. When our church invited the police chief to attend our "God and Country" Sunday service, he immediately accepted. He stated, "Your church's gift of prayer has meant the world to our officers."

||||||||||||||

Build Something. Take a team of construction workers, electricians, plumbers, and other helpers along with you, and physically erect a needed structure for a church. They may need help with repairs for the church or homes in the community. Plan well. Even better: raise money for the materials needed, and have materials ordered and on site before you arrive. Build a worship space, an orphanage, etc. Be sure to include some of the locals in the project and church members from that location as well. Add extras. Plant bushes or trees to finish the exterior. Order or make a nice sign. Raise money for furnishings for the building.

Disaster Relief Cleanup. Get trained by your denomination or local disaster relief group and be ready when disaster strikes. Your church can send a team of people to an area that has been hit by a disaster to help with clean up, pray with people who were affected, and counsel the survivors.

Feed the Homeless. Peanut butter and jelly are cheap. You can make tons of sandwiches and take them out to an area of town where there are many homeless families.

Sit and Talk. Is there an area in town, like a park, where people tend to hang out? Go there! Take lunch and a game to play. Pray and ask God to direct you to someone who is hungry for Him, and initiate a conversation.

‖‖‖‖‖‖‖‖‖‖‖‖

When we planted a church in England, we spent a large amount of time hanging out in the city park areas talking with people. It was amazing how much of a crowd we could draw by putting out games, starting a game of Frisbee or capture the flag, or even just by engaging people in conversations and inviting others in. Our little church was able to make a huge impact in our city by doing the very simple task of engaging in conversations about Jesus.

‖‖‖‖‖‖‖‖‖‖‖‖

Artist Missions Trip. Gather a missions team of artists, both professional and amateur, and another team to take care of other needs. Go to an "art hub" area, such as Los Angeles or Denmark. While there, connect with other artists, get involved with projects, and host classes and/or group projects. While the artists prep and teach, the others can spread out and do whatever it is God calls them to do to either invite people or discuss more important things. They can also get in on the fun while the projects are going on. You can go anywhere because art is a universal language.

Business Team. A missionary in an urban area might need a group of business leaders to facilitate a first-class topical conference for business or leadership development within their city. Host free seminars in the local church building for business people in the area. Incorporate Scripture and invite the attendees for worship service on Sunday.

Youth Rally. Hold a youth rally in the evenings to gather teenagers. Have a live band and a youth-friendly speaker (with translator, if needed). Spend time during the day ministering in the community and inviting youth to the big evangelistic event.

Family Missions Trip. Welcome everyone, from babies to grandparents, single parents, foster parents, and all types of family units. To accommodate busy schedules (as well as kids and the elderly who may not have extended amounts of energy) select a convenient destination and plan for a shorter trip, such as four days and three nights. Be sure to keep the schedule flexible and devotionals interactive and child-friendly. Select missions projects that allow children to work alongside their parents. Worship, work, serve, play, and learn together. It's a great time for parents to live missionally with their children and for cross-generational interactions and mentorship opportunities between church members.

||||||||||||||

We took our whole family on a missions trip to encourage International Mission Board missionaries in Spain and Portugal. Our church members led a great VBS and kids' musical. My husband, Steve, led Bible study, and we both had the privilege of spending time listening and counseling with each missionary couple. Our kids lived and interacted with missionary kids. As I reflect on that trip, though, I believe our own children were the greatest beneficiaries. They learned a different culture. They befriended missionary kids their own age, and still keep up with them to this day. And they learned firsthand about missions.

||||||||||||||

Age-Specific Ministry. A missionary may need a team to assist with reaching children, teens, college students, young adults, senior adults, or another age-specific group. For example, the missions trip may lead up to a huge, community-wide kids day as an evangelistic outreach. The earlier days of the trip may include several locations of Vacation Bible Schools, sports camps, parenting seminars, etc.

GET → GOING!

Whether you're a small or large church, begin to plan missions trips for next year right now. Your people will be blessed beyond their imaginations, and the missionaries you assist will be helped and encouraged.

Church Plant Project. Help a new church plant in North America or overseas with a specific project. If your church is partnering to plant a church, take a missions trip to help them. Consult carefully with the planting pastor, then determine what teams you can provide. (See more church plant missions trip ideas on page 55.)

Be ready for unexpected cultural differences. Lessons I've learned from missions trips overseas include:

In Sri Lanka, watch out for the monkeys—they throw things and follow you.

In England, the word pants refers to underwear—oops.

In Germany, apparently hamburger meat doesn't always have to be cooked.

In Indonesia, live grub worms are a favorite afternoon snack.

In Singapore, it's illegal to chew gum.

In many Middle Eastern countries, people greet one other with a kiss on the mouth.

In India, cows roam freely and are a part of the normal traffic flow.

In Italy, all drivers honk their car horns nonstop while driving.

In Spain, you may find yourself eating corn sandwiches and raw bacon.

In Mexico, you might be in a four-person taxi with 15 people.

In Canada, it sounds like everything's a question, eh?

In most of the world outside of America, they call "soccer," "football" and some drive on the other side of the road.

But there's one common fact in every country: people need Jesus.

chapter 5

ONE LONG-TERM MISSIONS IDEA

The harvesters are paid good wages, and the fruit they harvest is people brought to eternal life. What joy awaits both the planter and the harvester alike! You know the saying, "One plants and another harvests." And it's true. I sent you to harvest where you didn't plant; others had already done the work, and now you will get to gather the harvest. —John 4:36–38

f one hour, one day, or one week missions actions can impact our community and our world for God, imagine how He can use long-term missions projects!

Many of those shorter-term ideas in previous Chapters may easily evolve into effective long-term missions. Other community missions endeavors can best be done with an extended longevity in mind from the very beginning.

If your church's international missions trip is a fruitful success and you decide to return to help that missionary annually, that's long-term. When your church commits to being a sending church or a praying church for a new church plant, they usually help until that new church is self-supporting. When God calls some of our church members to be vocational missionaries, that commitment is usually long-term—for a summer, a year, or a lifetime.

Try a few of these long-term missions ideas.

FOR THE COMMUNITY
IIIIIIIIIIIIIIIIIIIIIIIIIIIIIIIIII

Some missions projects in your town are best done on a consistent, long-term basis. These established outreach ministries help your community see your church as a place of refuge and care.

English Learning Bible Class. If there is a population of immigrants who speak another language, begin a Sunday School class taught by a Christian who is fluent in the language. Teach the class in slow, simplified English for those who are trying to learn English. This becomes missional when your church members intentionally seek and invite outsiders to attend and include them when they come. Make an outreach plan to announce the kickoff for the class, then begin well.

Read to Children. Invite children in your community for an excellent weekly story time in the church library. Post story time hours on the exterior of the church. Provide bookmark invitations for members to invite unchurched neighbors. Recruit members who are great readers or retired teachers to make it a year-round community ministry. Designate a separate team of moms in your church to attend and visit with guest moms. Because it's consistent, you may list it in the "to-do" section of the local paper and on your church website. Capitalize on great Bible stories. Plan a summer reading program, with an emphasis on great Christian children's literature.

Truck Stops and Airports. If you're located near a truck stop or airport, ask permission to provide a worship service on Sundays. Some airports will allow you to use their chapel and advertise on the intercom. Create a team to provide an evangelistic, encouraging sermon, quality worship music, and a time of prayer with those who attend.

||||||||||||||||

An administrative assistant in our church hadn't finished high school and instead earned her GED as an adult. God led her to establish a GED ministry in our church, and a year later, several classrooms were packed full of students. Church members provided snacks for their breaks, and a different person shared a short, vibrant testimony while students ate. Many students received their high school diploma and, more importantly, many received Christ as their personal Savior. That's missions.

||||||||||||||||

GED Classes. Retired teachers or others in your church can lead. Advertise it well, and begin each class with an encouraging Scripture. Personally invite each student to your church worship service, and connect them with a small group. Celebrate with students when they pass their GED test.

Adopt a School. Your church or adult Bible class could intentionally help a nearby school. If your public school system is low functioning, your church can make an enormous difference. Visit the principal to offer assistance to the school for whatever they need. Be flexible, be consistent, and joyfully show God's love as you respond to requests.

→ Mentor or tutor students.

→ Volunteer in the office.

→ Read with students.

→ Serve as crossing guards.

→ Help students with scholarship applications.

→ Provide shoes, haircuts, or school supplies for a child in need.

→ Send encouraging prayer notes to the principal.

→ Provide after-school homework help or art classes.

→ Have snacks and mentoring available at the church one day a week after school.

→ Deliver snacks to the teacher's break room with a note from your church.

→ Paint the playground equipment.

→ Volunteer as classroom assistants.

→ Offer professional services free of charge: cleaning/janitorial, construction, grant writing, baking, etc.

Daily Bagel. A church in a low-income neighborhood could provide breakfast for children on their way to school. Many churches offer effective after-school homework help.

Military Mission. If there's a military base nearby, make it easy for soldiers to join you for worship. Offer transportation and friendship. Connect them with "host" families. Serve a weekly homemade meal at the church, with a great team of members to connect with them. As they are transferred or deployed, send them off with prayers and new friendships.

Missions in Gym Shorts. Create easy-entry gym events for outside guests. Use your website, social media, and printed invitations for church members to share, and outdoor signs to invite the community. Athletic church members participate regularly and use the opportunity as an evangelistic witness. Examples:

→ Singles volleyball night (or college, couples, etc.)

→ After-school gym hours

→ Pickup basketball games

→ Walking track, with early hours for senior adults

→ Exercise equipment

→ Open gym hours for families with kids on Saturday mornings, especially holiday weekends

→ Exercise classes, with Christian music and a two-minute devotional

→ Children's sports leagues, such as Upward Sports

→ Video game bowling for senior adults. Each team must have an unchurched guest.

→ Invite local firefighters and police department to use the gym and exercise equipment regularly.

||||||||||||||

As I added garlic bread to the plate of spaghetti, I looked around the small kitchen at the workers serving a weekly Sunday afternoon meal to about 90 homeless people. The church was small, but the volunteers were vigorous. Week after week, for more than five years, they provide transportation, a wonderful worship service, laundry, clean clothing, a hot meal, and kind words of encouragement. It's evangelistic. It's life-changing for many. They involve other churches. The ministry is one of the most awesome I've witnessed. My thought: this is one little line in this book of mission ideas—one line! Don't try to do 1,000 missions ideas (unless God tells you to do that). Find one, and do it well. Then find another, and do it well.

||||||||||||||

Foster a Child. Work with social services foster programs and group homes to care for children who don't have a home or have been removed from their home. Your church could encourage families to foster, and ask other members to encourage and help them. In the United States, there are almost 397,000 children living without permanent homes in the foster care system (ccainstitute.org). There are approximately 320,000 protestant congregations in America (2010 Religious Congregations Census). That means that if just one family in each church adopted one child, almost all children in the foster care system now could be placed in safe homes.

Hospital Missionary. Get permission from a nearby hospital for this ongoing project. Take a basket filled with treats and set it out where residents gather. Be sure to include a sign encouraging residents to take what they want, and include a message of God's love and your church's contact information. Our women's ministry group buys bulk snacks regularly, and seven ladies committed to deliver snacks on a specific day of each week. They replenish snacks, then sit and chat and encourage people there.

New in Town. Twice each year, begin a new small group Bible class for newcomers to your town. Advertise in the local paper or on social media, and ask members to deliver an invitation to new neighbors. Share information about the community and the church, and personally invite each guest to come to your church.

Move to Be on a Church Planting Team. Some members of the sending church may volunteer to personally be a part of the new church plant for a year. Others may join permanently. Challenge your church or small group to ask God if they can serve more permanently with the church plant. Are you a teacher? Businessman? Librarian? You can probably transfer to a city that has a church plant and keep working your same job, all while being a part of helping grow and serve a church plant! Think outside the box.

Refugee Ministry. Research or observe your own community to discover pockets of immigrants or refugees who have come to live there. That's a missions field for your church. Get to know them and find ways to show God's love. This type of ministry can enliven your own church! Some of these ideas could also be used for ministry in multi-housing or low-income communities near your church.

→ Help furnish their home. Many immigrants have few possessions.

→ Help them find work by providing contacts or an interview wardrobe, teaching computer skills, or even hosting a job fair.

→ Socialize with them. Assign immigrant families to church families. Invite them to your home. Have a barbeque with the entire group.

→ Assist with language. Simply providing conversation will help them learn English faster. Or, begin an ESL class.

→ Take time to get to know them. Learn their names. Be a friend. Give them a Bible in their native language. Observe interests, skills, and needs. Give a baby shower for a new mom.

→ Show love to their children. Give them a backpack filled with treats,school supplies, and clothing. Pay for them to attend church camp. Offer to help them with homework. Provide a safe place for them to play.

→ Help them find needed medical or dental assistance.

→ Teach them basic skills, such as grocery shopping or driving.

→ Plan a ladies lunch for all the ladies.

→ Provide for needs, such as box fans, clothing, and food.

→ Help them prepare for U.S. citizenship requirements.

→ Many immigrants are poor, but others are professionals. Church members in similar vocations (doctors, technicians, etc.) can intentionally befriend them. Show God's love in tangible ways, and share His story of salvation.

||||||||||||||

Carlos was ten years old when his family fled communist Cuba with nothing but the clothes they wore. Southern Baptist Convention's North American Mission Board (NAMB) helped the refugee family find a home and a church. Christians showed God's love to the refugees, and Carlos accepted Christ as His own Savior. He grew into a great man of God, a successful accountant, and for the past 23 years, Carlos Ferrer has served as NAMB's chief financial officer. Refugee ministry changes lives.

||||||||||||||

Give Bibles. Make a long-term plan to give a Bible to occupants of every home or apartment in your town, county, or subdivision. Purchase the Bibles, map your route, and make assignments. Chat with each neighbor and invite him or her to your church. Write a note inside the Bible, suggesting they begin reading in the Book of John and inviting them to your church. Even better, deliver each Bible with a flower from members' gardens and the Scripture, Isaiah 40:8, "The grass withers and the flowers fade, but the word of our God stands forever."

Prison Ministry. Begin a worship service or a mentoring program at your local prison. Share Jesus and disciple Christians. Provide counseling. Consult with a prison chaplain or visit a prison in your area to discover ways your church can minister there. Begin or attend a worship service there. Assist with prisoner education programs.

Families of Prisoners. Be creative in ministering to prisoners and their family members. Plan ways to minister to inmate families when they come to visit. Do a project to provide gifts for inmates' children, such as Angel Tree (prisonfellowship.org/about/angel-tree). Work with the chaplain to find ways to contact and assist family members who live in your immediate community. Develop long-term relationships to serve and encourage them. A church in Texas staffs a building outside a prison where families awaiting a prisoner's release can relax. They offer information, materials, encouragement, and prayers. What a ministry!

Minister to the Abused. Create a halfway house or a women and children's shelter.

||||||||||||||

A very small church in Indiana has one of the most effective women's shelters we've seen. Size doesn't limit effectiveness when God calls.

||||||||||||||

Assisted Living. View local nursing home facilities as a great missions field. Select one nearest your church, or one where a church member resides. Arrive before the ministry time, and spend time chatting and listening to residents. Pray with them. Be intentional about sharing Jesus verbally with them and never assume they know Him already. Whatever ministry idea you choose, be sure to add a testimony about God, and present the gospel. Try some of these ideas:

→ Monthly birthday parties
→ Tuesday tea
→ Paint fingernails
→ Weekly Christian music. Bring your band or quartet, and have fun.
→ Organize a video game bowling league
→ Bingo
→ Weekly worship service
→ Offer a Bible study about heaven
→ Holiday parties, especially religious holidays

Read the Word. If you read aloud for 30 minutes a day Monday through Friday at a slow, steady pace, you can read the entire New Testament in about three weeks. Find one or two residents who would enjoy that, then obtain permission and get started. Plan to hang around and visit afterward for a few minutes. Several in your group could visit the center once each week. Include your children in the visit. Both the residents and the children will be blessed.

More Assisted Living Ministry. You may want to choose a low-income assisted living center where needs are great.

→ Give small laundry baskets in the winter season filled with necessities such as sweatshirts, blankets, toiletries, etc.
→ Take a stack of new pillows and pillowcases for each resident.
→ Purchase groceries or basic household items to donate and deliver to each home.

→ Use the holidays as an excuse to lavish residents with holiday decor items for their rooms/apartments to make it festive.

→ Gather donations of fuzzy blankets and deliver one to each resident with an encouraging note.

Deliver Newcomer Baskets. Sometimes people who have relocated are more open to learning about God. A friendly team can deliver a small gift and personal invitation to worship. Use a newcomer list, or ask church members to call the church office when someone moves into their neighborhood. Ask newcomers if the church can help them in any way. Be alert for ways to show God's love.

Senior Adult Students. Many universities provide free tuition for senior adults. If yours is a senior adult small group, encourage members to register for a class that interests them, and be intentional about building relationships and sharing Jesus with other students.

John replied, "If you have two shirts, give one to the poor. If you have food, share it with those who are hungry." —Luke 3:11

Disaster Site. Be prepared and offer your church as a staging site during crisis. Have a plan to quickly involve the majority of church members in ministry. If the damage is great, this could be a long-term commitment.

Block Party Trailer. Your church, or a group of churches, may invest in a portable trailer, rigged up with popcorn and cotton candy machines, balloon animal supplies, bounce houses, puppet theater, stage, sound equipment, etc. It's an instant party to transport to an apartment complex, park, neighborhood, or event where you'll attract people and share Jesus.

City Ball Team. Put together a team and register for a city league sport with the intention of sharing Christ with the other teams. This could be softball, bowling, rowing, tennis, or any sport with a league. Pray together before each game, asking God to give opportunities to share about Him. Show great sportsmanship, play your best, have a great time, and treat the competition with respect. Be sure your banner or shirts state that you're from the church. Be intentional about creating witness opportunities. For example, your team invites their opponent to meet at the ice cream shop after the game.

English as a Second Language (ESL). Research to discover immigrants who live in your community, and connect with them. Participants learn basics of English language grammar and American culture through group lessons and then volunteers in the church spend time weekly with the class in casual conversation. God might even lead you to start a small group or Bible study in their native tongue as a way to be on mission through the ESL program.

Benevolence Ministry. Set up a donation system at your church where members donate gently used clothing and nonperishable food items. It could be an organized closet in the church that's open two hours per week, or a whole building with multiple ministries. For every benevolence ministry, your plan should include evangelism.

Help a Benevolence Ministry. If your church doesn't have one, consider volunteering long-term to assist a like-minded church or ministry to the needy. For example, if a church in your community serves the homeless every Sunday afternoon, your small group could offer to help cook and serve on the first week of each month.

Feed the Hungry. Some churches serve hot meals or soup to the hungry. Consider long-term ways to feed the hungry of your community.

Add More Benevolence. Be sensitive to needs and add ministries. Examples: soup kitchen, Christmas toy shop, Thanksgiving meals, cooking or nutrition classes, thrift store, computer skills classes, business attire assistance, language help, interview skills training, culture skills training, parenting classes, and friendship. Share God's plan of salvation.

Care Clinics. Establish a free health clinic or dental clinic as a ministry to the poor. Your registration or discharge plan should include sharing Jesus.

Juvenile Missions. Talk with your county's juvenile probation department to ask how your church can help. They may need mentors, sports coaches, or other volunteers. One church works with a juvenile judge who assigns community service hours to troubled teens and often sends them to volunteer at the church's benevolence building. The church is intentional about praying for, befriending, counseling, and encouraging these young people.

Sermon Delivery. Does your church have a few people who live in a nearby nursing home? Stop by after church with a copy of the bulletin and a CD or DVD of the service. Purchase a CD or DVD player if they don't already have one. Visit with them, let them know you are praying for them, and give them an update on what is happening at the church. Remember to speak positively about the church and its leadership as you ask them to continue praying for the church. Encourage them to invite their neighbors in the nursing home to watch or listen to the sermon with them. Help them know how to share the gospel with those who come.

Teach Them to Read. An estimated 10 percent of adults in the United States read below a functioning level. Literacy training can open a new missions field in most areas. Offer classes or one-on-one reading instruction, and share Jesus.

Good Neighbor. Make a yearlong plan to deliver small gifts to each home within a specific number of blocks from your church or in a target neighborhood. Begin by delivering a Bible and invitation to church, then plan delivery to each home every other month, such as a small flag on July 4 week, a little pumpkin for fall, or a bookmark for Mother's Day. Converse and make friends. Each delivery could have a church brochure or invitation to an upcoming event at church. The final delivery is a nice invitation for Church Neighbor Day (see page 82).

Addiction Support Group. According to the American Hospital Association, one in four Americans are affected by a mental illness or substance abuse disorder each year. There are likely many in and near your church. Begin a God-focused outreach program to offer hope and help, and welcome them into your fellowship.

Know Your Neighbors. Really. You might build relationships that will last a lifetime instead of just waving as you leave for work.

➡ Take one year to invest intentionally in those who live directly adjacent to your home.
➡ Make a chart and keep it on your refrigerator. As you learn the names of each neighbor around your home, write their name and info on your chart so the whole family can memorize their names.
➡ Call them by name any time you see them.
➡ Invite them over for dinner, or suggest going out to dinner together.
➡ Offer to babysit their kids on a date night or invite them to join you at the park for an afternoon.
➡ Be a friend. Establish a relationship. Listen as you chat for ways to show God's love and share how He's impacting your life. Share Jesus.

Prison Bible Correspondence. If there is not a prison nearby, research a prison Bible correspondence plan. Very effective! You'll grade their studies, write personal comments and encouragements, and help lead a prisoner to Christ or disciple him or her.

Adopt a College Student. Many college students would love to have a family away from home. You or your small group can provide this for them while they are away at college in your town. If you know a Christian coach at the school, your small group could offer to individually "adopt" a player on that team. Show God's love and encourage your student. Examples:

➜ Offer to let them do laundry at your house.

➜ Cook a homemade meal.

➜ Be available to help when they have a flat tire or need a ride to the airport.

➜ Share Jesus with the student.

➜ Be a mentor.

➜ See the Adopt an International Student idea below for more ideas.

Adopt an International Student. Ask God to help your group see the missions field of college students from other countries who study in a school near your church. Many of these students have never been in an American home or heard the gospel. Here's a way to do foreign missions without having to learn a new language, travel across time zones, move away from family and friends, get lots of shots, live under the threat of imprisonment, or eat unfamiliar food! God has brought internationals—many of them from countries that do not allow missionaries—right to your very doorstep. Call your local university's international office, and meet with the director to ask how your small group or church can help. They may pair families with international students while they are studying in the states or provide other ministry opportunities.

→ Invite them to your home for holidays (they probably can't travel home to be with family anyway).

→ Take them out to the county fair.

→ Treat them to a fancy restaurant in town.

→ Buy them a Bible.

→ Be a friend. Hang out. Laugh. Listen.

→ Help them with cultural challenges.

→ Help them find things in the grocery store.

→ Assist with transportation.

→ Host them for dinner.

→ Bring them to your church on Sundays.

→ Help them with the language barrier.

→ Provide furniture or household goods.

Off-Site Worship. Start an off-site Bible study or worship for people who can't come to church. Be faithful and see this as a long-term commitment. Look around and see where God wants you. Consider:

→ A local prison

→ Fire department

→ Your home

→ A beach Bible study or worship service, if you're near the ocean

→ An evangelistic worship service for tourists in a nearby state park

→ A nursing home

→ A truck stop

→ A hospital chapel

→ A rodeo arena for cowboy church

→ An area where many homeless reside

→ An airport chapel

→ A ship ministry, for cargo carriers or cruise ships

→ Oil workers. Baseball players. Golfers. Look at your community and see people who might not otherwise find God.

Sports Ministry. Start an Upward Sports program in your church gym or field (upward.org). This program teaches children basic sports skills and sportsmanship, and gives you an opportunity to share Jesus each week.

Purposeful Upward Fans. Your senior adult class or other small group could make plans to attend the entire season of an Upward Sports program. Arrive early, sit with parents, cheer like crazy, and enjoy the games. Volunteer in the concessions stand or man the scoreboard. Learn the children's names. Purposefully converse with parents and spectators, knowing that many of them are unchurched. Take every opportunity to invite families to worship and Bible study, and talk about your Savior.

||||||||||||||

The boy had just signed up for our church's Upward basketball team when his family discovered that his dad had cancer. The coaches, players, and church ministered to the family faithfully. One by one, each member of that family became a Christian. The dad's funeral occurred before the Upward season ended. At the awards ceremony, the little boy received the coveted Spirit award.

||||||||||||||

Trafficking Ministry. Talk to local law enforcement for ideas of how your church can minister to local sex trafficking survivors. One church provides a home-cooked meal in a motel's lobby where many immigrants arrive. They have been trained to carefully observe for signs of trafficking.

Shoeboxes or Christmas Toys for Kids. Your group may create an annual tradition of collecting shoeboxes for overseas ministry, such as Samaritan's purse, a similar local ministry, or toys for needy children or prisoners' children. Make the project fit your community and church missions field, and be sure there's a follow-up plan for Christian impact. For example, one church prepares shoeboxes for children in a school in the poorest section of their own town. They work with the school counselor, and children know it's a gift from God's church. Another church group has resources to purchase a bicycle for every first grader in their local, lower-income school. They are given as a gift in Jesus' name!

|||||||||||||

The Appalachian ministry of our denomination collects stuffed backpacks for some of the poorest children in our country. One little girl, who received the very last backpack that day, was twirling around with her hands in the air. "Thank you, God, for my pink coat!" she sang. She'd prayed to God for a pink coat, and that's exactly what was rolled up in her new backpack.

|||||||||||||

HOA Supporter. Join your neighborhood homeowners association. Actively attend meetings and be helpful in the conversations instead of complaining. Over time, make a reputation as a caring person who knows God. If possible, join the board or leadership of the association to invest on a larger scale.

Select Three. Choose three (or one or ten) neighbors on your street or apartment complex and determine you'll do one thing for each of them each month this year. Pray daily for each of them. Ask God to show you opportunities to serve them.

→ Help hang outdoor Christmas lights.

→ Take homemade cookies.

→ Offer to babysit.

→ Smile and chat with them.

→ As you interact and connect with them, find ways to talk about God.

Mission to Missionaries. As a church, consider buying and furnishing a house for furloughing missionaries. Be sure to establish relationships with those missionaries.

Bleacher Missionary. If your spouse, children, or grandchildren play sports, talk with your family about the opportunity to be a Christian witness to players and their families.

→ Watch and listen for needs. Seize every opportunity to show God's love.

→ Sit with different people.

→ Learn their names—the parents and the kids!

→ Keep church brochures in your car's glove compartment.

→ Invite them for a special event at church.

Community Garden. Provide a community garden with individual plots for gardening. Members garden there, too, and interact with community members to share Jesus' love. Spend time getting to know other gardeners. Learn their names. Learn their spiritual conditions. Talk about how God works in daily life. Be sure every gardener is invited to your church for worship.

Backpacks for Kids. All year long encourage church members to donate new school supplies, backpacks, jeans, T-shirts, etc. Hold a community event for needy families just before school begins inviting them to come "shopping" at the church for their school needs. All items are laid out on tables and displayed beautifully around your fellowship hall. Have a host walk with each family and generously give them the items they need for school this year. Remember, the whole point is to give away the items—be sure not to embarrass anyone who asks by graciously giving in Jesus' name. Have an area where your children's Sunday School teachers can meet families and invite them to church after they gather their supplies. Maybe you could have the host walk the family down the children's hallway and show them their age classroom and where to go for worship. Give them a printed invitation before they leave, and pray with them for a great school year.

Adopt an Area of Town. For an entire year, plan multiple missions trips to a specific neighborhood in your community. Block parties, holiday events, cookouts, clean up days . . . get creative in ways to serve the community as you share the gospel. Have a goal of starting a small group Bible study in one of the homes of that community or in the local park. It's amazing what can happen when you focus on one area and continue to go back and build relationships with the people who live there serving them and sharing Jesus.

Adopt a Struggling Church. If there's a church in your area with meager resources, find out how your church or small group can help. Your assistance could make an eternal difference.

Nearly-Wed Seminar. Invite every engaged couple in town to attend a multi-week seminar during Sunday School hour. Each session is a topical Bible study about marriage, with homework and handouts. At completion, couples get a certificate and are promoted to the newlywed class. Too much for your church to do multiple weeks? Make it a weekend event, offering marriage counseling, relationship building activities, and practical assistance. Staff a booth at the local bridal fair to advertise the class. Each weekly class addresses relevant topics from God's Word. Make it fun and informative.

||||||||||||||

Our church discovered an unexpected "missions field" in our community. We advertised heavily through social media, word of mouth, and a booth at our town's largest bridal fair to invite engaged couples to an excellent eight-week nearly-wed class. The class was repeated annually and met Sundays at 9:30 a.m. to coincide with our church's other small groups. Class registration was enormous every semester, and it drew many couples who didn't know God. Topical classes taught biblical answers, and each couple was assigned a mature Christian couple as mentors. Many future brides and grooms met Jesus, and couples were "promoted" into the newlywed couples small group.

||||||||||||||

Long-Term School Mentoring Ministry. Connect with the nearest public schools to volunteer for ongoing mentoring with struggling students. Get permission to wear your church name tags or T-shirt so students recognize they are working with members of your church. Spend time each week with students helping with homework, reading, or math skills. As you help the struggling student, be intentional about showing them God's love. This can be a great ministry for retired or future teachers in your congregation.

After-School Care. See the missions field of children in a nearby school. Some possible opportunities:

→ Supervised recreation in a gym, playground, or weight room.

→ Establish a program so kids can earn a scholarship to summer camp.

→ Homework tutoring. College students and retired teachers may enjoy this mission.

→ Leaders encourage school achievement and attendance.

→ Teach children to read and help them love to read.

→ Provide access to books. Consider a story time for younger children and chapter books for older children.

→ Offer summer classes and homework help.

→ Assist with college applications and scholarship applications.

→ Organize field trips.

→ Offer fun learning classes, such as acting, improvisation, theater skills, public speaking, diction, languages, drawing, painting, sculpting, computer graphics, dance, music lessons (vocal, guitar, drum, piano)

→ Organize intramural sports teams that anyone of any athletic level can participate in.

→ Offer artistic classes: painting, drama, creative writing, or choir.

→ Serve a hot meal or healthy snacks.

Every Christian's Missions Field. Where do you spend time? That is exactly where God has placed you to be on mission for Him. Consider every place you spend time, and be intentionally on mission for God there. Here are some examples:

→ Walk your dog? On mission to other dog-walkers and neighbors

→ Jogger or marathoner? On mission to other runners

→ Business traveler? On mission to each airline seat mate and flight attendant

→ Avid shopper? On mission to salespeople and fellow shop-a-holics

→ Foodie? On mission to greeters, servers, and fellow eaters

→ Office worker? On mission at the water cooler

→ Gamer? On mission as you play with others online, sharing Jesus through your attitude and words

→ Parent Teacher Organization member? On mission to every teacher, administrator, and parent

→ Social media buff? On mission to your followers and friends

→ Clubs and organizations? On mission to every other member

→ Golfer? On mission to teammates and competitors

→ Mom? On mission at the playground, stroller track, or moms group

→ Homebound patient? On mission to everyone who comes to your home, such as postal carrier, repair people, visitors, home health workers, etc.

→ Carpool mom? On mission to each person in your automobile

→ Subway or bus rider? On mission to fellow riders

→ Student? On mission to every teacher and fellow student

→ Hospital patient? On mission to others in the waiting room, roommates, doctors, nurses, medical technicians, food deliverer, volunteers, guests

→ Exerciser? On mission to the adjacent stair-stepper

GET → GOING! *Begin long-term missions projects and plans right in your town.*

FOR MISSIONARIES

We've acknowledged that every individual Christ follower is commanded to go and make disciples wherever he or she lives. God calls some, however, to vocational or volunteer missions, leaving everything they know and moving to live long-term in a place God calls them to serve. Others are called to serve for a shorter amount of time—maybe a year or two overseas or a summer helping a church plant.

How has God called you to be a part of missions? Jesus referred to us as the sheep of His flock and said, "My sheep hear My voice, I know them, and they follow Me" (John 10:27 HCSB). Isaiah 30:21 says, "and whenever you turn to the right or to the left, your ears will hear this command behind you: 'This is the way. Walk in it'" (HCSB).

God's people hear His call because He is a loving Shepherd ready to give direction that is best for us! Are you listening? Are you asking?

God may call you to live on mission for Him exactly where you are currently. He could call you to be a full-time vocational or volunteer missionary. You could serve on a stateside church plant team or an international missions team. You could do a one- or two-year missionary assignment. You could be a student missionary for a week, a semester, or a summer. God might send you to serve as an intern with a planter or missionary in a largely unchurched city. He may call you to spend retirement on a missions field. You might be a chaplain, an evangelist, or a teacher. God is calling you to be His ambassador, His missionary. The possibilities are endless.

Ask God today to send out missionaries from your own church and small group. Be prepared to joyfully give your best people to God's work—or to be the one who is sent. Help those He calls to vocational missions succeed.

Regardless of how God calls you, your family, your small group, or your church to be involved in long-term missions, we can guarantee this: you won't regret saying "yes" to His call! Here are a few ideas of ways you can be involved in long-term missions:

HELP PLANT A CHURCH IN NORTH AMERICA

America is a vast missions field. One of the most effective methods of reaching the lost in the United States is to plant churches in high-density cities that have few evangelical witnesses. Your church can be a part of the church planting movement! Any church can plant. Small churches plant churches. Large churches plant churches. Church plants plant churches. The various levels of partnership to help a church plant can range from prayer partners to financial supporters and everything in between.

All over the United States there are churches planting churches. It's easy to think, We'll plan to do that once we get bigger, but the reality is, no matter what your size, you can be a part of planting churches! Our church plant has a tiny annual budget, a small membership, and doesn't even own a building, but we are actively involved in raising up church planters and working to send out teams to plant churches. Even as we write this book, we just prayed out a team of people who planted a Chinese church in our area. There is no church too big or too small to plant—so begin a plan now to see how your church can be involved in reaching the lost.

||||||||||||||||

Assist a Church Plant. Consider helping with a church plant in one of North America's most populated and least churched cities. Study your denomination's plan for church planting, and ask God to direct where to help.

Be a Sending Church. Some denominations call this a parent church or a sponsoring church. This church provides wisdom, accountability, stability, and encouragement for the plant until the new church is self-sustaining. The level of financial assistance and other help varies.

Plant a Church with a Group of Churches. There may be multiple churches who partner to help in various ways.

Be a Strong Prayer Partner for a Church Plant. Make a serious commitment as a church to pray for a specific new church plant. Learn about their missions field. Meet the church planter. Read their newsletter or updates. Every Bible class, every choir rehearsal, every meeting or dinner or ball game is another chance to pray for that church planter and team.

Plant a New Church in Your Own Church Building. If you've discovered an unchurched people group in your community—especially a language group—consider planting a new church right in your building. This works great because they have a very interested sending church (where they meet), and meeting facilities are often an enormous roadblock for church plants. For example, a large population of Burmese people was discovered in Indianapolis, so a Burmese speaking church was planted using the facilities of a nearby established church. At one time, our church had a Vietnamese, Hispanic, and Arabic church all meeting in our church building at different times. Each one became a self-sufficient church over time.

||||||||||||||

A small church in Cumming, Georgia, has three non-English-speaking church plants that meet in their church building at different times. Each church has its own church planter/pastor. Yes, there is some sacrifice in sharing your church facilities, but what a generous gift to help a church get started.

||||||||||||||

Pray for a Planter. Have your small group "prayer adopt" one of the church planters your church supports. Every week when you meet as a group, take focused time in prayer for the church plant. Keep an eye on their website, social media, or newsletters for prayer points. Any church plant would be delighted to have many committed prayer partners.

Go to a Church Plant. Does your church have a partnership with a church plant already? It's very important for members of the sending church to physically attend worship there occasionally, even if it's across the country.

||||||||||||||

Our church planted two new churches within driving distance and asked all members to worship with one of those church plants at least bimonthly. The plants were always encouraged to have members of their sending church join them for worship and the sending church was encouraged that their support really mattered.

||||||||||||||

Join a Church Plant. Ask God to call out a quality individual, couple, or family (or several!) from your church to physically relocate and help the church planter. They move to the church plant city, find jobs, and invest heavily in the life of the new church.

IIIIIIIIIIIII

One church sends a different volunteer team every two months to help with a project and to worship with their church plant 1,000 miles away! It could be the pastor, a family on vacation, or a couple with the sole plan to encourage the church plant. I'm in awe of people from sponsoring churches who actually relocate their family temporarily or permanently to help plant a church. If God leads, will you invest a day, a year, or a lifetime?

IIIIIIIIIIIII

Serve in their Kids' Ministry. Volunteer to be in the nursery or children's ministry for the first six months of the new church's Sunday meetings, or for special events. This will give the church time to grow together as a family and raise up leaders in their congregation to take over the children's ministry.

Join the Church Plant for a Year. If the church plant is across town from you, consider membership there to help them get started. One couple from our sending church joined us for a year, faithfully attending and working.

Join the Church Plant Long-Term. Volunteer to be part of a church plant long-term. Find a job in the area where the new church is located, buy or rent a home, pay your own way, and be a vital, working, effective part of the team.

IIIIIIIIIIIII

When you help plant a new church, you may be amazed at its long-term effect. Last month, we were invited to help celebrate the new worship center at a church we planted decades ago. What a taste of heaven! The hotel where we stayed was a few miles from church, and as we checked out that morning, we noticed a church plant setting up for worship there. We chatted with the enthusiastic group and learned that their sponsor church was a church plant that had been planted by our church plant. Grandchildren! What a blessing.

IIIIIIIIIIIII

Volunteer to Lead a Bible Study for Your Nearby Church Plant for a Year. Give it your best, and disciple others to take your place. Invest your retirement years by attending and serving in a church plant or on the international missions field. Contact your denomination's mission-sending entity for complete list of opportunities.

GET→GOING!

Invest hard into helping a new church plant. Your assistance can make an enormous difference.

Send Interns. Students and members from your church can serve short-term or summer-long internships at a church plant in the states or overseas.

|||||||||||||||

Our parent church in Texas helped our Oregon church plant by conducting a phone survey that the church planter pastor designed. Those canvassing questions resulted in several initial members of that church. Imagine using Internet surveys or social media to help from across the country.

|||||||||||||||

FOR LONG-TERM INTERNATIONAL PARTNERSHIP
||||||||||||||||||||||

Declare His glory among the nations, His wonderful works among all peoples. —1 Chronicles 16:24 (HCSB)

Your church group may be taking an overseas missions trip. But, instead of a single-shot trip to help a missionary for a week or two, consider a longer partnership. If God directs the missionary and the church alike, make a long-term plan for more missions trips and creative ways to enhance that mission. Some churches set a specific time period, such as a three-year partnership, and then evaluate to consider an extension.

There are many benefits of a long-term relationship with a missionary:

→ Your church will develop a relationship with the missionary.

→ Your church will find a great love for that missions field.

→ Some of the same individuals may make multiple trips as relationships are established.

→ Your various trips may be similar or radically different.

→ Some individuals in the church who travel for business or pleasure might make a visit there to help or encourage.

→ In many instances, your long-term relationship will earn the right to share Jesus with the people in the area.

→ Be sure there will be follow up after your missions trip. The most desirable method is to partner with a missionary who is serving in that place, especially a missionary supported by your denomnation or church. Check with your denomination. Make a contact. Ask if your church could partner with that missionary.

→ Partner with a missionary your church supports. If your denomination or individual church trains and supports missionaries, your missions trip will further enhance that relationship.

GET → GOING!

Plan missions trips across the world, and help a vocational missionary as a long-term partner.

|||||||||||||

It was our third missions trip to teach high school English in a small town in East Germany. The first year, our team of college and older high school students were given a half day in the public school, each day for a week, to teach English as a second language. We used crafts and visuals to tell about American holidays and culture. They allowed us to freely share the Christian meaning of those holidays and invite students to the evening "Jesus Nights" at a church nearby. They came in droves! Even the teachers. The principal and teachers were so enchanted with our students' joy and the German students' response to them, they invited us to return and teach half a day all week the next year. The next year, we were allowed to teach the entire day of school for a week. We built relationships with students, faculty, and the local church. More than a decade later, the church where we served still sends a missions team to that same school and church in Germany. Long-term partnerships are effective.

|||||||||||||

Missions in a Crisis. Some unplanned situations open doors for long-term missions partnerships. Disaster relief, both in North America and internationally, often requires long-term assistance.

|||||||||||||

In 2005, our church in Texas sent multiple short-term teams and a long-term team to Sri Lanka after the tsunami a year earlier. Over the course of the following years we adopted one area and helped the people to completely rebuild their village and begin new businesses. A group from the church worked with the women in the village to turn the old roof tiles of their homes that had been destroyed in the tsunami into beautiful sconces that they then sold online to finance building materials to rebuild their village.

|||||||||||||

"For the Good News must first be preached to all nations."
—Mark 13:10

chapter 6

ONE CHECKLIST FOR MISSIONS TRIPS

hen a church or small group plans to impact their nation or their world using short- or long-term projects or trips, the most fruitful method is to partner with an existing missionary in that locale. Not only will that missionary save you time and errors, but the labors can be much more fruitful as that missionary can follow up with new believers and pursue doors that have opened as you've served there.

Consider partnering not just for one trip, but also for a few trips. As you return to one location over and over, your church will in turn grow a heart to reach those people and have wonderful overseas relationships to invest in.

> *Finally, brothers, pray for us that the Lord's message may spread rapidly and be honored.*
> —2 Thessalonians 3:1 (HCSB)

SELECTING THE PLACE TO GO

Your tithes and offerings already support missionaries monetarily. Will you put a "face" on missions and personally connect with at least one missionary? Pray, pray, pray. You might be surprised where God leads your church. Don't rule out anything—let God speak, and look into every option. Some of these ideas may help you determine your mission destination.

> *So we decided to leave for Macedonia at once, having concluded that God was calling us to preach the Good News there.* —Acts 16:10

Befriend a Missionary. Establish a connection with a missionary who came from your church or your denomination. You'll have an immediate bond and can build easily on that.

As You Go. Connect with a missionary in a state or country where members of your church travel for business or pleasure. If Jenna travels regularly for work to Dubai, a missions partnership would be enhanced there. She could check on the missionary or deliver needed materials. If the McDougald family visits New York twice a year for vacation, a missions partnership with a church planter there would be a natural fit.

International Congregants. Connect with a missionary who serves in a home country for some of your church members. Perhaps they migrated here, or their heritage is in that country.

Visit Your Church Plant. If your church is helping plant a church in North America, try to take at least a couple of missions teams to assist that church planter each year.

Support a Missionary. Connect with a missionary who came from your town or state. Inquire at your denominational office to find one. You may be surprised to discover missionaries who came from your area and now serve across the nation or world, supported by your denomination!

Follow Up With Visiting Missionaries. Connect for a missions trip with a missionary who has spoken in your church.

Partner With a Local Missionary. Encourage a missionary who serves nearby in your state—i.e. a church planter, collegiate minister, or chaplain. It will simplify ways you can encourage him or her. Get to know them and encourage them.

Utilize Denominational Resources. Contact your missions-sending denominational office for suggestions of a missions trip destination with a missionary, a church planter, or an unreached people group.

Play to Your Strengths. Consider the skills and interests of your congregation and find a location that fits. Do you have a lot of artists? Plan a trip to Europe. Do you have a lot of builders? Plan a trip to a developing country. Take athletes on a missions trip where a sports camp would be helpful to the missionary there.

Count the Costs. Be aware of the economics of your own church as you consider a location. Be aware of travel and housing costs and how that might affect the amount of people who would be able to participate in missions. For example, a plane ticket from Indianapolis to Kiev, Ukraine, might be double the cost of a ticket to Mexico City or Anchorage, Alaska.

Reaching the Unreached. Adopt an unreached people group, and make a long-term plan to share Jesus across the world. Your mission-sending denomination can connect you with an entire people group who has no evangelical witness. Plan to send teams to that same location repeatedly. This will build your church's heart for that area of the world and give you long-term impact in a location.

Missionary Home. Consider buying and furnishing a house in your town for furloughing missionaries from your denomination. Establish a long-term relationship with families who stay there, and consider planning a missions trip to help them.

Research. Read everything missions-related from your denomination's missions boards. God can use those stories to help you select a missionary to assist.

Health Assessments. Consider health restrictions of your potential missions trip participants. Many European countries require extensive walking and stairs, which could limit the people you can take.

On the Go. Where do your people already go? If several of your church members tend to vacation in Colorado, plan a family trip there and connect with a local church.

||||||||||||||||

From childhood, I lived in the Bible Belt. I married a pastor and church planter, and we served over 30 years in Texas. When we moved to the Midwest, the biggest culture shock was not the customs or the weather; it was the scarcity of evangelical churches! Can you believe it? North America is a great missions field, and thousands of church plants are urgently needed, especially in the highest-population, least-churched parts of our nation.

||||||||||||||||

INVOLVING THE WHOLE CHURCH IN THE TRIP
||||||||||||||||||||||||||||||||||||||||||||||||||||||||||||||||

When you plan a missions trip, share the blessing with your entire church.

Prayer Pals. Get a team of prayer warriors who will pray during the entire planning process and as you travel. The week before and during the trip, provide some type of prayer reminder, such as a plastic bracelet with one team member's name.

Involve Kids. Ask a children's Sunday School class to write individual notes to children you'll work with. (Or teens, if you're working with teens, etc.)

Supply the Team. Ask the women's ministry group to collect needed items, such as candies for children, small appropriate gifts for women, craft supplies for a kid's day, VBS decorations, etc.

Welcome Home Plan. Whether you're arriving at the airport or the church, secretly plan a welcome home for the group. No refreshments or program, of course. Just a big homemade sign, maybe a couple of balloons, and people who love them shouting, "Welcome home!"

Notes and Prayers. Is a group from your church going on a missions trip? Write encouragement notes for the team and deliver to the team leader. Offer to coordinate a group to gather and pray for them every day while they are gone.

Consider the Needs. Make provision boxes for your church team going on a missions trip in a needy area. Research the needs of the community they will serve, and fill boxes according to those needs (cooking oils, soap to wash clothes, beans, etc.). Consider the expense of transporting those pieces, if the group is traveling by air.

Encourage the Team. Ask a small group or class in your church to prepare a small goodie bag for each team member before you leave. Make it small enough that they can put it in their carry-on bag (and remember not to include anything that would get them in trouble at the airport—no liquids, sharp objects, etc.). Include some snacks, a puzzle book, pen, and an encouragement card saying, "I'm praying for you."

Assembly Line. Ask for volunteers to help staple booklets, prepare witness bracelets, etc.

Personalized Support. Think of the different groups in your church—choir, sports team, deacons, senior adult group, and so on. Be intentional about involving them in support that fits their interests and gifts. The choir might video themselves singing a song in the language. The deacons might purchase a nice Bible for the church planter or pastor, signing it individually with promises of prayer. Make it fun, and report back to those who assisted after the trip.

MAKING PREPARATIONS/CHECKLIST FOR THE LEADER
||||||||||||||||||||||||||||

Communicate Effectively. Communicating with your contact (missionary, pastor, missions trip coordinator on site). Have one primary contact person from your group communicate with one primary contact from the missions site. Fit the ministry with the needs of the missionary on site. Listen carefully. Remember that you are serving them, not the other way around. When you make that initial phone call, your offer should be, "We would love to come serve you—however that looks." Be sure to let them know what your people are capable of doing, but to call a missionary and say, "We will come and do this," isn't very helpful. Your plan of VBS or choir presentations may not work in their context. Listen carefully to know if your group is best suited for the area you are looking to serve.

Consider Participant Requirements. Every trip is different, but every team should be intentionally chosen. If your trip is out of state or out of the country, you want to make sure that your team members can spiritually, emotionally, and physically handle the trip. Here are a few things to consider as you choose your team:

→ Should this trip be customized for participants of a certain age?

→ Can families with children come to this location?

→ Can they physically handle this location/project? Think through the travel, accommodations, and what you will be doing. Many missions trips are physically demanding and might rule out people who have difficulty handling extraneous movement. A team of all high school girls wouldn't be best for a trip where you will be building a church. Instead, take the men's group on this trip.

→ Are they ready in terms of maturity level? You might want to rethink taking a middle school missions trip to a dangerous area. Leave that trip for college age and older.

→ Where are they spiritually? Going on a trip to Europe can be incredibly difficult spiritually. People in Europe tend to have very deep questions and are strong in their approach. Taking a spiritually immature individual might do them more harm than good in their own walk with God, depending on your location.

→ Do they have stringent diet limitations or food allergies? Many countries are incredibly food-oriented. To turn down their offer of a meal or to demand specific foods will be very disrespectful and could destroy your witness.

Consider Having an Application Process. Prepare an application packet with all the details on where you will go, what you will do, the dates, the cost, and what type of people you are looking for to be on the team. In this packet, be sure you include the dates of your training days as required attendance for the team. Have a portion that they fill out and return to the team leader by a certain date. Then, have a committee of people who gather the applications, pray through them, and determine the team for the trip. A few things to have on your application are:

→ Full legal name and birth date (you will need this when ordering airline tickets).

→ Passport number (If this is an out of the country trip, they will need to have their passport in hand well before the trip date. It's ideal to already have one at the time of application.)

→ General contact information.

→ Questions to determine spiritual maturity level. For example, "How consistent is your individual time in the Word of God and prayer?" "What is something God has been teaching you in the Bible lately?"

→ Questions to determine their desire for this mission. For example, "Why do you want to participate in this missions trip?"

→ Questions concerning their physical health, physical ability to travel, and food allergies.

→ If you have a specific purpose for the trip (ex. building, medical, art trip), ask how their unique skills will contribute to the team.

→ For minors applying, have a section for their parent or guardian's signature on the application.

The Leader's Checklist.

☐ Where will you stay?

☐ Who will you work with?

☐ What can your team not do? What are your limitations?

☐ What will are the requirements for being on the team? (Spiritual, physical, emotional maturity?)

☐ How often will you need to check in with your pastoral leadership while you are gone and how do you need to do that? (E-mail, satellite phone, cellphone, or land line?)

☐ How many people can you take on the trip? Consider travel and housing arrangements, your capacity to shepherd the team well, and adult sponsors if needed.

☐ Tie a brightly colored ribbon on every person's bags and carry on items for ease of identification at pickup.

☐ Print an emergency card for team members to keep with them on the trip. List pertinent info such as address and phone for the missionary, church, and American embassy.

☐ Consider ordering or planning one item that identifies your team for the trip. A printed T-shirt, ball caps, bandanas, etc. This will come in handy.

☐ Consider seating team members individually on the airplane with an assignment to tell their seat mate about their trip and their God.

☐ The evening before the team leaves, invite parents/friends/prayer partners/supporters for prayer. Mark all baggage with matching ribbon and load as much as possible beforehand.

☐ The foreign missionary where you're traveling for your missions trip may have difficulty receiving supplies or personal items by mail. Let them know ahead of time that if they'd like to order some things (home school materials, book, personal interest items) and have them delivered to your home, you'll be glad to deliver them in person.

☐ Ask the church planter or missionary what items he or she can't obtain where they live. A Ukraine missionary jumped with joy when we brought his favorite beef jerky from the States. As you plan, listen carefully to know the missionary personally and bring a gift or two that will be meaningful. If it's not in your personal budget, ask your small group at church to help you purchase it. And, of course, it must fit in your luggage.

☐ It seems small, but if the missionary is not able to find printed media in English where they serve, they'll enjoy anything you bring. Take magazines, current books, and a newspaper. Many missionary families with children would be delighted to have books or DVDs of television shows and movies appropriate for their families. If you're not sure, ask.

▮▮▮▮▮▮▮▮▮▮▮▮▮▮▮

On one trip we all took three of our favorite books or CDs to leave with the missionary's family. Their teenage children thanked us over and over and were so excited to have something new to read and listen to.

▮▮▮▮▮▮▮▮▮▮▮▮▮▮▮

☐ Don't Forget the MK. If the missionary has children (MKs), wouldn't it be nice to take a special gift for them?

▮▮▮▮▮▮▮▮▮▮▮▮▮▮▮

The daughter of a missionary where our team served loved art. Our team chipped in to buy her a small personalized wooden box of art supplies. She was delighted! And since she had to share her parents and her home with us during the trip, she definitely deserved a nice gift.

▮▮▮▮▮▮▮▮▮▮▮▮▮▮▮

TRAINING YOUR TEAM BEFORE YOU GO
▮▮▮

For every missions trip, you need to be prepared, both practically and spiritually. Use these tips for creating team training days for your missions team to prepare them for the upcoming mission. Make the training days are required for everyone going on the trip. This will ensure that everyone is properly trained and will also give the team time to get to know each other before you leave.

As the leader of the missions team, you should put a lot of effort into these training days. Remember: the smoother these days go, the smoother your trip will go! Plan ahead and be prepared to make these days fast paced and jam packed with info your team wants (and needs) to know, and keep it fun!

Team Member Testimony. Have everyone on the team share his or her five-minute testimony. Keep a timer handy and keep people to five minutes or this could go on forever! It's great for everyone to have a grid of where the others on the team are coming from spiritually. Also, this is a great time for you as leaders to take notes so you know how to minister to your team members as you go. This will further instill the expectation of team members to be able to effectively communicate their relationship with God.

Strengthen Team Relationships. On each training day, include a team building exercise or two. You can find examples online that will give you options for different games and activities to build your team. Before you choose one, think through your team and what they need together—are they a group of strangers who need to get to know each other? Are they a group of friends who need to learn how to get along better? Do they need to learn how to communicate with each other or work together? Let these "needs" drive the team building exercises that you choose.

Learn About Your Missions Destination. In your first training day for the trip, divide your team into pairs and give each pair a research topic. Instruct them to take a few weeks to study their topic and come back to the next training day prepared to give a five- to ten-minute presentation to the group about what they learned. Handouts and visuals are always helpful in teaching people. Some topics could include:

➡ City facts (statistics on the city/country you will be serving)
➡ History of Christianity in your location (How have people in your location responded to the gospel in the past?)
➡ Current state of Christianity in your location (How do people view the church now?)
➡ Other religions and cultures in your location (Are they majority Muslim? Catholic? Buddhist? What drives their world view?)

→ Language differences (Do they speak English? If so, is it the same as you? Do they use different slang words and phrases? If they don't speak English, what are some key phrases and words to know before you arrive?)

→ The church you are serving (Study what their church mission is, who their leadership consists of, and how they are currently reaching their community.)

→ Weather and money exchange rates

Visualize the Future. Find videos and photos of your location to share with your team so they have a visual grid of what the people and culture look like there.

Meet Your Missionary. In one of your training times, set up a video chat meeting with a contact in the state or country where you will be going. Have them share with your team the types of things they can expect when they are on the trip. Even simply hearing the accent of the contact will be enough to fill your team with excitement. Have the team ready to ask questions and pray for the person you chat with—to be an encouragement to them as they help administrate your trip.

Establish Team Friendships. Plan break times throughout your training days where people can laugh together, get to know each other casually, and process some of the information you are teaching them. During these breaks, provide snacks that are from your trip location as a fun way to introduce them to the culture. If you are going overseas, you can find a lot of snacks from other countries at your local grocery store or a multicultural home goods store in your area.

Worship Together. Take a significant amount of time to worship and pray for the church and location you will be serving. Give God the time and space to break your hearts for the lost in that area.

Talk Practical Details. People get most nervous when they feel unprepared or uninformed. Give them as much information as possible. This includes details about your schedule, where they will stay, dates and times of travel, when finances are due, and what they are responsible for as a team member.

Open Q&A. Always leave plenty of time for questions. Your team will have lots of questions, even after training days. You may not have all the answers, but at least you can show them that you are preparing well and can find answers to questions you're not sure about. Their questions will probably really help you in your planning as well, to think of things you haven't considered yet. Be sure you do have the answer to their question by the next training day.

Personality Tests. Some people love them, some people hate them. Regardless, conducting some sort of personality test and talking about it together will help your team better understand one another. More importantly, it will open their eyes to understanding that everyone does not respond to situations the same way they do. You can find free tests online. Be sure to have time to talk through what each personality type is and how that will affect the way that person responds on a missions trip. For example, a team full of introverted people will likely need to have some time "off" during the course of your trip to get refreshed and re-energized. A team of extroverts will require a lot more planning on the part of the leadership to be sure they are kept busy. A team with both (most likely your team) will need to be aware of each other's needs and look out for each other in this way.

Evangelism Preparedness. Do extensive training on how to share the gospel and how to share your testimony. Make sure this isn't just sitting in a room training—actually go out and do it. Knock on doors in your neighborhood together to share the gospel, go to the grocery store and pray with people you meet. Challenge every team member to share the full gospel with at least one person per week from that day

177

until the day you leave. Be sure in your next training time to go around and have everyone share about his or her experience doing this for accountability and extra training. Remember, if you're not doing it at home, you won't do it on the missions field.

What to Pack. On your last training day before you leave, be sure to give your team a packing list. Help them know what to bring and (more importantly) what not to bring. People tend to over pack on missions trips—packing light is always key.

Behavior Modification. Do a cultural sensitivity training. What is the culture like where you will be ministering? Are they a loud, boisterous culture? A quiet, reserved culture? Help your team know ahead of time how to be sensitive to this as they go. For the most part, Americans are known for being loud and annoying in other cultures. Train your team to be sensitive to the people around them—not singing on the train, walking on the correct side of the sidewalk, proper behavior in a worship service, etc. These things might seem like common sense to you as the leader, but the excitement of being in another culture or the pride of being an American can easily overtake a team and diminish its effectiveness in ministry.

Go With the Flow. Missions trips rarely go as planned. Teams need to be flexible and ready to do whatever is asked of them. We tell our missions teams that their motto for the trip is, "Where you lead me, I will follow. What you feed me, I will swallow!" In the training times, plan in times of structure that you intentionally "mess up." Give the team feedback on how they did in handling the change with flexible attitudes.

A Cheerful Giver. Give expectations for the team's behavior and attitude on the trip. Make a behavior covenant and have everyone sign it saying they understand how they are expected to behave on the trip. This really helps you as the team leader when someone is out of line on the trip—you can easily pull him or her aside and lovingly remind them of the covenant they signed.

Planning Meetings = Serious Preparation. Divide into teams to accomplish some tasks. Schedule meetings and rehearsals ahead. Give lots of written details. At the first planning meeting, distribute pipe cleaners or bendy toys to each person on your missions trip team. Ask them to describe the item. Let them know from the very beginning that "flexibility" is a key ingredient to any successful missions trip. One of our missions teams even made "flexibility" T-shirts to wear at meetings! Use long pipe cleaners. Ask team members to bend them into something to represent themselves, and then introduce themselves with it. Then ask the entire group to attach their pipe cleaners together to form a circle, and talk about the importance of being flexible as a team.

Leave It All Behind. If your missions trip is to an extremely impoverished area, plan to wash and leave all your clothes and shoes except what you're wearing home.

Add Music. Find a theme song that resonates with your missions trip purpose. Sing it often.

Hostess Gift. Consider gifting your host or hostess with an item specific to your home:

→ American candies
→ A T-shirt or water bottle from your local university
→ Anything with an American flag if you're going overseas—magnet, pen, coasters, kitchen towels, etc.

Set the Standard. As the leader, don't ask your team to do anything you wouldn't do. Be an example and work in the trenches with them.

Pull Your Own Weight. Make a hard and fast rule: if you bring it, you carry it. Every person must carry and load their own luggage. Limit personal baggage to be less than the required airline amount. Your team will want to bring home souvenirs and won't be thinking about that extra weight when they pack initially. You'll often need team members to check an extra bag of supplies for the ministry.

AS YOU GO
||||||||||||||

Take advantage of every opportunity to teach your team as you are on mission.

Stay Connected. Plan to have a one- to two-hour team meeting every morning on your trip:

→ Take time to worship together each morning.

→ Give the team practical details they will need for the day: schedule, resources, expectation, etc.

→ Have someone from the church you are ministering to come and share in each team meeting. They can share their testimony, give a devotional for the day, or use this as a cultural training time.

Culture Training. Do it often! Ask good questions of your team such as, "What is something that you notice that is really different here from home?" "What is your host home like?" "How are you doing with navigating, walking, or riding public transportation everywhere?" These questions begin culture conversations and give you insight into how your team is doing.

Pray Continually. Take a good amount of time to pray together for the day. Seek God for His direction as you minister to people.

Minister to Hearts. Keep your eyes open as you lead the team and watch for team members who are having a difficult time. As the leader, don't be afraid to pull someone out of a ministry activity to go for a walk and help them process what's going on. Some people really have a difficult time when they are away from comfortable surroundings and might need time to process instead of waiting until you get home to walk them through things. Be aware of your team's needs.

Be a Local. Take a fun day and go see the city. Ask the locals what is the best thing to do or see in town and go do it—just budget it in before you leave. You want your team and your church to not only fall in love with the church they are serving but to fall in love with the city they are serving as well. Fun days accomplish that and also give your team some much needed mental and spiritual rest.

Mid-Week Checkup. Schedule in some discipleship time with your team. Consider having one or two times (depending on the length of your trip) where you break up into a men's group and a women's group and give people time to share what God is teaching them and doing through them on the trip.

Utilize Downtime. Take advantage of built-in time (vehicle rides, waiting for the next project, waiting at a bus or train stop, etc.) to communicate with your team.

AFTER YOU RETURN HOME
||||||||||||||||||||||||||||||||||||||||||||

Host a Debrief Meeting. This can be done each evening during your trip or on your way home on the bus, at a restaurant, or in the airport. Or, schedule a meeting at your church the week after you get home.

Share Digital Photos. Create an online account for all of your team members to share their photos with each other when they return.

After-Party. Schedule ahead (put it on your trip calendar) to have a party a week after you get back home. The team will be missing each other by that point and will enjoy getting together and retelling all of the great stories. Invite team members to bring supporters and family members. Have some food and snacks from the place you served. For example, if you went to Canada, serve a native dish, such as *poutine* (it's sort of like French fries with gravy and curdled cheese).

GENERAL TIPS
||||||||||||||||||||||||

A Clean Sweep. Be aware of how your team can help the church in the downtime between projects that may come on missions trips (i.e. clean, sweep, etc.).

Rejoice Always. Require a good attitude at all times from your team. No exceptions.

Be Attentive. Listen and be receptive to needs.

Gather Daily. Have team meetings and devotions daily. Give the team plenty of time to process what they are experiencing together (not only after you get home).

Capture the Moment. Take an action photo of each team member demonstrating servant leadership or ministering to someone in the community. E-mail that photo to the team member after the trip.

No Church Is Too Small. If you think you're not big enough for an over-seas trip, pair with other small churches to take a missions trip. Or join another church on their missions trip. Talk with associational leaders or nearby pastors to learn about opportunities.

IIIIIIIIIIIIIIII

Sitting in the Mexico dirt, painting a little girl's fingernails, I realized our missions team was doing exactly what the missionary needed. It was a simple crowd-gathering event set up in front of a church member's adobe home. Our team played music, cut hair, played games with children, chatted with people, and served tortillas. People came from all over the neighborhood. Each hour, a bell clanged, and the missionary shared the gospel. A few people accepted Christ as Savior, and many got to know the missionary as a friend. Over the next months, many of them accepted Jesus, too. On our next visit to Mexico, we found several of those new Christians joyfully following Jesus.

IIIIIIIIIIIIIIII

Pray as You Plan. Be intentional as the leader to make prayer a necessary requirement of your team. And not just for you! Call on your team members to pray out loud multiple times throughout and leading up to the trip. Have them pray in front of the whole group or pray in twos and threes. God wants to hear from you as you go—don't forget to talk to Him.

→ Begin and end every meeting with prayer.
→ Assign prayer partners among missions trip participants.
→ Pray before the flight.
→ Pray when God blesses during the trip.
→ Pray when problems arise.
→ Pray and praise after trip.

Experience the Culture. Add a fun day at the end of your trip. Take the missionary with you and pay their way for the whole day if at all possible (buy their lunch, their museum ticket, travel costs, etc.).

Dear Mom. Especially if it's more than two weeks, find a way to communicate home. If possible, send group updates to all family members of your team a few times a week instead of having individuals call home.

Post Updates. Consider posting photos every few days on a social media page or church website with an update about what God is doing.

Video Chat. Give team members the option to video call with their family one time on the trip.

Full-Focus Missions. Watch out for social media. If the team has constant connection to what is going on at home, their hearts and minds will be distracted from what God is doing in and through them on the trip. Consider a "no contact with home" rule. Give relatives emergency contact information to get a hold of you as the team leader if they absolutely need to speak with someone on the team.

|||||||||||||||

No missions team ever got to the field and said, "Well, we over-prepared."

|||||||||||||||

Share Your Life. Ask each participant to prepare a small photo album to help them share their lives with hosts, especially on overseas trips. Share photos of family, pets, school or work, your small group at church, your ministry at church, and hobbies. Don't show wealth. Show joy.

Integrate Your Church. Consider doing a live feed from your missions site on Sunday. Your small group or even your church might enjoy a video chat from your missions team on site. Make it strictly two minutes long!

Expect the Unexpected. Be ready in season and out! You never know what might be asked of you when you go to serve in another area. Train your team and prepare yourself for anything. You might be asked last minute to preach on Sunday, lead worship for a small group, or run a kid's camp. The best missions trips are always the ones where the completely unexpected happens and creates an amazing space for God to move.

▐▐▐▐▐▐▐▐▐▐▐▐▐

When I was in India, our hosts caught wind that I was a youth leader in America, and I was asked to come and speak at a youth evening for an international youth group. Not knowing anything about it, I agreed and was taken in a rickshaw over to the other side of town to a really nice hotel. What they did not tell me was that this was the final youth evening of the school year, and all of their families were also invited. On top of that, the youth in this group were all the children of the country ambassadors to India. With no preparation time, I was placed to speak in front of a captive audience of the ambassadors and their whole families from 75 different countries. You'd better believe I was glad that I came prepared to share the gospel boldly!

▐▐▐▐▐▐▐▐▐▐▐▐▐

Keep Them Posted. Consider posting an update or short video online every couple of days. Assign who will do these. Show the terrain, buildings, culture, but concentrate on what God is doing—show people, prayers, and smiles. Doing this on a social media site allows your team members to easily share the video update with all of their friends without distraction from their focus there. The more people who see the update, the more people you will have praying for you as you serve! Once when we were in Ukraine, the missionaries we assisted posted an ongoing story of the team's ministry on their blog, along with a photo or two. Team members linked that to their e-mail list or Facebook so family and friends could be on mission with us.

||||||||||||||

On our most recent missions trip to England, we had a college student who served as our team videographer. All day long, he took videos of the team working on projects, sharing the gospel with people on the streets, and serving the local church, then he would spend the late night hours making a 60-second video of the day and posting it on our church's social media page. Of course he also participated in the ministry of the trip, but the video updates were his main job on the team. Those videos had hundreds of views every day and helped our family and friends back home keep us in constant prayer while we were on mission.

||||||||||||||

chapter 7

ONE BIG PLAN: GO!

cross the Street and Around the World was written for one purpose: to ignite a missions fire in your heart and help launch your small group or church to go outside your church walls.

As you've plowed through these hundreds of missions ideas, we hope you've repeatedly thought, "We could do that!" We hope you've had exciting discussions with other Christians about the potential for doing missions because God created you for this.

Our prayer is that you've begun to look around at your own community, seeing it with a fresh perspective as your personal missions field. As you drive through your town, you notice people you didn't even see before. At work, read your e-mails with a new, upward focus. You see simple ways to add an intentional missions purpose to some things you're already doing. You see needs, hurts, and lostness surrounding you. You see people groups and children and senior adults who don't know God. You pay attention to world and local news differently—with eternity in mind and a prayerful heart of compassion.

Imagine how your small group would look if everyone began to live on mission. Picture how your church would change if you helped plant a church in an unreached part of North America. Or if your church adopted an unreached people group across the globe. Imagine how

God could use your work, travel, or vacation time as a missions opportunity. What if your church planned missions trips to unengaged areas of the world and to the city a few hours away from you? Are you excited yet about the potential of purposeful missions trips to spread God's Word and help vocational missionaries?

There's a smoldering spark of excitement. You are ready to go.

With all of this information you've just taken in, here are ten simple tips to help you get started as you put feet to what God is stirring in your heart.

PRAY
IIIIIII

You know that living on mission is God's will. Stay on your knees asking for God's wisdom and guidance as you follow Him. Don't be overwhelmed with all the ideas suggested in this book. Just pray for God to show you one single missions project, then another, then another. If you lead a small group or a church, ask the entire group to pray for God's direction.

> *So we keep on praying for you, asking our God to enable you to live a life worthy of his call. May he give you the power to accomplish all the good things your faith prompts you to do.* —2 Thessalonians 1:11

> *He said to his disciples, "The harvest is great, but the workers are few. So pray to the Lord who is in charge of the harvest; ask him to send more workers into his fields."* —Matthew 9:37–38

GET THE BIG PICTURE
||||||||||||||||||||||||||||||||||

God already has a fantastic plan to take His good news to the world. It's you. God created you to tell others about Him. If every church and small group and individual in every town began to live on mission, can you imagine the wildfire of salvations that would happen?

Missions opportunities abound. Realize that these hundreds of starter ideas are just a tiny tip of the iceberg of missions opportunities God has ahead for your church or small group. Your greatest missions idea may not have even been mentioned between these pages! But the harvest is plentiful, and when you begin to see your world through God's eyes, He will show you great missions fields.

If you lead a small group or a church, share Scripture, websites, and printed materials with your group to get them informed and envisioned for missions. Ask some leaders to skim this book and write their comments about possible ways for your group to be on mission. Get the big picture as God sees it. Remember, "When people do not accept divine guidance, they run wild" (Proverbs 29:18). So give your group the compelling guidance of God to reach the unreached.

You saw me before I was born. Every day of my life was recorded in your book. Every moment was laid out before a single day had passed. —Psalm 139:16

You didn't choose me. I chose you. I appointed you to go and produce lasting fruit, so that the Father will give you whatever you ask for, using my name. —John 15:16

Based on the gift each one has received, use it to serve others, as good managers of the varied grace of God. —1 Peter 4:10 (HCSB)

If you try to hang on to your life, you will lose it. But if you give up your life for my sake and for the sake of the Good News, you will save it. —Mark 8:35

THINK BIG
||||||||||||||

*May he give you the power to accomplish all the good
things your faith prompts you to do.* —2 Thessalonians 1:11

What's the biggest thing your church or small group could do to spread
the gospel to those who don't know Him? If there were no limitations
on resources or time or people or money, how would your group share
Jesus? If God is leading your group to a specific missions project, such
as planting a church or welcoming immigrants, read every resource
about it. Tap into your denomination's resources. Ask God for wisdom
to accomplish that big vision. Everyone everywhere needs Jesus. This
is big.

If you are a leader of a small group or a church, pray to your great
God who created the world and has limitless resources. Ask Him to
give you, as the leader, a great vision for missions in your community
and around the world. Ask Him to help you cast a big vision for those
in your group to live intentionally on mission for Him daily.

*And then he told them, "Go into all the world and preach
the Good News to everyone."* —Mark 16:15

*We cannot stop telling about everything we have seen
and heard.* —Acts 4:20

*But the believers who were scattered preached the Good
News about Jesus wherever they went.* —Acts 8:4

MAKE A PLAN
|||||||||||||||||||||

Go back through the notes you wrote as you read this book. You've
marked dozens of potential missions projects that your church or small
group could accomplish over the course of this year. Prayerfully ask
God for leadership as you decide where to start, but make a plan to

start soon. What missions ideas prick your heart most? Which ones do you feel would fit your church or small group well? Is there a common theme? Do some opportunities seem to be an obvious, exciting choice for your church or small group?

As the pastor of a church or the leader of a small group, listen carefully to members of your group. Has God given some of them a heart for a specific ministry? Is someone concerned for the homeless in your town? Does someone have a great desire to take a missions trip to a developing country? Use those natural desires and giftings that God has put into your people to develop missions project and trip ideas that best suite them specifically. Be sure to put dates on the church calendar as soon as you decide what to do so the maximum amount of people will be able to participate. Wisely delegate, and help gather people and resources to launch missions projects and trips as God leads.

A small group may decide to do a different missions project together monthly. Or they may discover one ongoing missions focus they love. They may plan seasonal missions projects in the community or may organize a missions trip to help a church planter or international missionary.

Start with a one-hour project or a local missions trip, and watch your group or congregation's vision grow into something bigger. Your group might be completely overwhelmed by the idea of going on mission to Haiti, but put together a trip to a neighboring state first and you can capture their hearts for reaching the lost close by, then gradually work up to a more challenging trip.

Regardless of how you plan your missions focus, every church has huge potential to impact the world missionally. Many churches appoint a missions committee to help oversee and uplift missions action. Some hire a missions pastor. Some do both! Others simply get together with their small groups and ask, "What are we going to do this month to be on mission?"

Any size church can plan ways to be on mission in their community. Any size church can help plant a church in an unreached area of North America. Any church can plan a missions trip to help an international missionary or a church planter. No matter its age, size, or location, your church was created by God to be on mission for Him. But you have to be specific and make a plan or your missions ideas will always remain only ideas.

> *But I have raised you up for this very purpose, that I might show you my power and that my name might be proclaimed in all the earth.* —Exodus 9:16 (NIV)

> *"For I know the plans I have for you," says the LORD. "They are plans for good and not for disaster, to give you a future and a hope."* —Jeremiah 29:11

> *For you are to be his witness, telling everyone what you have seen and heard.* —Acts 22:15

> *Make the most of every opportunity in these evil days.* —Ephesians 5:16

GATHER A TEAM

Your team might be a single age group, a small group, a cluster of families, or an affinity group. Maybe a team of doctors, carpenters, or teachers. Maybe a group of all three! Be specific and intentional about gathering a team that is dependable and willing to serve in Jesus' name.

Pray about who to ask to join your team on this mission. Should it be an "all call" or a specific invitation to individuals? Should they be strong believers who you can trust, or can a first-time visitor join in on this project or trip? As a church or small group, plan multiple trips and events this year to accommodate all of these groups so that everyone can participate in missions.

TRAIN YOUR TEAM
||||||||||||||||||||||||||||||

See Chapter 6 for specifics on training your team, and don't underestimate the importance of being prepared. Every missions project needs good preparation and execution, but your team will be so much more confident and secure as they go out on mission if they feel like they know what they are doing.

Have practice days for where you will go and what you will do. Practice sharing the gospel with one other. Practice teaching the Bible study time or leading music for a kids Vacation Bible School. Give people ample time to feel prepared.

GIVE IT YOUR ALL
||||||||||||||||||||||||||||||

In your small missions endeavors, give it your best. In your large missions enterprises, give it your best. There is great joy in doing God's will. Do it with all your being. Go wholeheartedly. When we accomplish the mission God has assigned us, it gives life great meaning.

> *But my life is worth nothing to me unless I use it for finishing the work assigned me by the Lord Jesus—the work of telling others the Good News about the wonderful grace of God.* —Acts 20:24

If you're the leader of a small group or a church, lead the way. As you serve on mission for God, do it with joy and enthusiasm. Consider seeking wisdom and direction from a church leader around you who is already leading their group in this way. Ask them to pray with you and for you as you lead your group to do the same. Ask them to challenge you personally in the area of missions and evangelism in your everyday life. Keep in mind that whatever you are not doing where you currently are is exactly what you will not do wherever you go. So, start practicing today! Go out and share the gospel with a stranger at a gas station this week. Start a conversation with your next-door neighbor today and invite them to your church or small group. When your group sees you living out what you are calling them to do, they will be significantly more excited to jump in and follow your leadership to the ends of the earth. It begins with you as the leader walking forward on mission with an undivided heart, leading the way.

> *Whatever you do, do it enthusiastically, as something done for the Lord and not for men.* —Colossians 3:23 (HCSB)

> *I do everything to spread the Good News and share in its blessings.* —1 Corinthians 9:23

> *But you should keep a clear mind in every situation. Don't be afraid of suffering for the Lord. Work at telling others the Good News, and fully carry out the ministry God has given you.* —2 Timothy 4:5

> *We loved you so much that we shared with you not only God's Good News but our own lives, too.*
> —1 Thessalonians 2:8

TRUST GOD

Don't fret. You can relax now. When you're doing what God's called you to do, He will give courage, protection, and peace.

If you're the leader of a church or small group, lean hard on God. Demonstrate trust in your great God, and lead others to trust Him as well. Trust Him to direct you where you should go and what you should do. Trust Him to handle roadblocks. Trust Him for the financial provision for your project. Trust Him to lead you to an area full of people who are hungry for Him. Trust Him for protection and safety as you travel. Trust Him for wisdom on handling the ups and downs of serving together as a team.

Each church we've served has planted churches. We often wondered how we could afford to send out members to these new church plants—what will that do to our church in terms of leadership and finances? But God has always provided. In fact, each time we'd plant a new church, our own church would have a growth spurt as well. People get excited and begin to trust a church that is willing to see the gospel go out, no matter the cost. So set the example and trust Him.

> *Again he said, "Peace be with you. As the Father has sent me, so I am sending you."* —John 20:21

> *For we are God's handiwork, created in Christ Jesus to do good works, which God prepared for us to do.* —Ephesians 2:10 (NIV)

> *This same Good News that came to you is going out all over the world. It is bearing fruit everywhere by changing lives, just as it changed your lives from the day you first heard and understood the truth about God's wonderful grace.* —Colossians 1:6

> *You know how badly we had been treated . . . and how much we suffered there. Yet our God gave us the courage to declare his Good News to you boldly, in spite of great opposition.* —1 Thessalonians 2:2

> *God will make this happen, for he who calls you is faithful.* —1 Thessalonians 5:24

BE PURPOSEFUL
IIIIIIIIIIIIIIIIIIIIIIII

As you set out on each mission, remember that your ultimate purpose is to point people to know Jesus as their personal Savior. Every mission is in His name alone.

If your goal in doing missions is to make yourself look good, that's the wrong purpose. If you're concerned with getting your name in the local paper or the church bulletin, that's the wrong purpose. When your key focus is to magnify God and make Him known to those who've never met him, that's missions!

As a church or small group leader, be certain the focus of every missions project or missions trip is on Jesus alone. Train your team to know how to share their personal testimony and the full gospel. From day one of planning the trip or project, make it clearly known that this is all about people being invited into relationship with Jesus.

> *Those who are wise will shine as bright as the sky, and those who lead many to righteousness will shine like the stars forever.* —Daniel 12:3

> *When you produce much fruit, you are my true disciples. This brings great glory to my Father.* —John 15:8

> *And whatever you do or say, do it as a representative of the Lord Jesus, giving thanks through him to God the Father.* —Colossians 3:17

> *Christ's love controls us.* —2 Corinthians 5:14

GET OUT THERE
IIIIIIIIIIIIIIIIIIIIIIIII

Most importantly of all, take action immediately because the task is urgent! We have no guarantee of tomorrow, so today is the day to start making your plan and go out on mission.

> *Teach us to number our days, that we may gain a heart of wisdom.* —Psalm 90:12 (NIV)

> *We must quickly carry out the tasks assigned us by the one who sent us. The night is coming, and then no one can work.* —John 9:4

Never be lacking in zeal, but keep your spiritual fervor, serving the Lord. —Romans 12:11 (NIV)

Indeed, the "right time" is now. Today is the day of salvation. —2 Corinthians 6:2

Sharing Jesus with our community and our world is too important for us to wait. Jesus' instructions did not say, "Huddle inside the church building and wait for all of the instructions to clearly know where I am calling you and what I am calling you to do there." He didn't say, "Go into all the world next year when you plan your annual church calendar and budget." He didn't say we should go after retirement, when we're young, or after we've made our fortune. God calls for every believer, everywhere, all the time to go now.

→ If you're a seminary student preparing for full-time ministry, you must be going daily as you study.
→ If you are a brand new Christian, go.
→ If you're a teenager or college student, go.
→ If you're young or old, single, widowed, divorced, or married with children, go.
→ If you are rich or poor, go.
→ If you are in prison, in military, in Congress, in debt, in a band, go.
→ If your church is tiny, go. If your church is huge, go.
→ If you've focused inward instead of outward in the past, turn around and go.
→ If your church or small group is stagnant, declining, or dead, wake up and go.
→ If your group is alive and vibrant, go.

Then I heard the Lord asking, "Whom should I send as a messenger to this people? Who will go for us?" I said, "Here I am. Send me." —Isaiah 6:8

CONCLUSION

But be doers of the word and not hearers only, deceiving yourselves. —James 1:22 (HCSB)

y brother has a three-year-old daughter, and she is learning how to fish. I love seeing the photos he sends of her casting her fishing line out into the swimming pool and patiently sitting on the deck. She is getting good at practicing and tells us all about how good she is at fishing. But let's get real—she hasn't caught a single fish. She's fishing in the wrong place for maximum impact! Isn't that how we as the church often approach missions? We're really good at practicing, but it's time we put on the waders and get in the river where the fish are.

Jesus called out to them, "Come, follow me, and I will show you how to fish for people!" —Matthew 4:19

Now that you've read some super simple one-hour missions ideas, huge missions challenges for international partnerships and missions trips, and everything in between, we pray that you will wholeheartedly reach out to the folks around you in Jesus' name. As your small group or church begins to intentionally live on mission outside the church walls, God will bless your service. Missions begins at our door and extends through the streets, across the nation, and around the world. Pray for the Lord of the harvest to send out workers. Beginning with you.

So, at the risk of sounding a bit like Dr. Seuss—

Go on.
Get out there.
Do something.
Skedaddle!
Get up, go out.
Live for something that matters!

You were created for this! It's time for the church to leave the building and go from one idea to a thousand ideas—now take it and go! It's no longer just about the gathering . . . it's about the going.

But you will receive power when the Holy Spirit comes upon you. And you will be my witnesses, telling people about me everywhere—in Jerusalem, throughout Judea, in Samaria, and to the ends of the earth. —Acts 1:8

APPENDIX

MY COMMUNITY QUESTIONNAIRE

ow can your small group or church be on mission for Jesus right here in your community?

If you're just not sure, this form can help leaders of your small group or church immensely. Complete every blank, using factual data from sources such as census .gov, your city website, your city library, denominational research, and Chamber of Commerce statistics. Notice there is a space beneath each question for you to fill in. If you still have empty blanks, keep digging. Answers on this form may unveil a missions platform.

As part of this process, divide a city map into sections, and assign different leaders to drive or walk every street in that grid. The goal is to observe and prayerfully ask God to help us see our city as a true missions field, in need of Him. They may walk into office buildings or ethnic stores, sit in the park, or stop by a coffee shop or fire station. One or two leaders could visit the mayor, school superintendent, and police chief to ask these three questions:

What do you see as the top three needs of our town?

What major changes do you see on the horizon, and what challenges or opportunities will they bring?

What do you feel our church could do to help improve the quality of life in our town?

Afterward, everyone can meet back together to pray and ask God to inspire ways your small group or church can be on mission for Him. Carefully review stats and notes. Brainstorm ways God might use your church members' influence, history, gifts, and interests to be on mission in your community.

Most importantly, don't just talk about it. Read the first word of the Great Commission in Matthew 28:19–20 (HCSB). Go!

MY COMMUNITY QUESTIONNAIRE

City/town population

County population

Largest employer in town

Number of people employed at largest employer

Average commute time to work

Median age of residents

Average number of preschoolers

Average number of elementary age children

Average number of teens

Average number of young adults

Average number of senior adults

Popular pastimes of residents

Crime stats

Most frequent crime

Products made in your town

Three largest annual events in town

Percentage of single adults: list divorced, never married, widowed

Something your town is known/famous for

Average summer and winter temperatures

Ethnic percentages/breakdowns

Largest major disaster in town history

Unique residents, i.e. drill workers, military, medical students, etc.

Poverty level/Poverty pockets/Needs

Area growth or decline last year

Biggest news item in town last month

my community questionnaire

Biggest news item in town last year

Most popular pastimes in your area

What is unique about your town?

Ethnicity mix/Ethnic pockets

Languages spoken

Percentage of lost or unchurched in town

GO CHART →

OUR GREAT COMMISSION STRATEGY

Acts 1:8 calls us to go to our Jerusalem, Judea, Samaria, and the ends of the earth. Contrary to popular belief, this isn't an order of how ministry should happen. It doesn't say, "start in Jerusalem, then go to Judea . . ." The intent is for it to all happen simultaneously! So how is your church or small group engaging all of these areas simultaneously?

	WHERE?	WHAT IS MY CHURCH DOING IN THIS AREA?
MY JERUSALEM (MY OWN COMMUNITY)		
MY JUDEA (MY STATE)		
MY SAMARIA (MY NATION)		
UTTERMOST PARTS OF THE WORLD (MY WORLD BEYOND MY NATION)		

WHAT IS MY SMALL GROUP DOING IN THIS AREA?	WHAT IS MY FAMILY DOING IN THIS AREA?	WHO ARE PARTNERS WHO CAN HELP?

GO CHART →

RETHINK ACTS 1:8

Or . . . rethink Acts 1:8 in terms of people instead of geography. All four of these could be in your own city. Geography never makes someone a missionary. Acts 1:8 is about more than just geography, it's about people. Think of it this way. . .

	WHERE?	WHAT IS MY CHURCH DOING IN THIS AREA?
MY JERUSALEM (PEOPLE I KNOW, WHO ARE LIKE ME)		
MY JUDEA (PEOPLE I DON'T KNOW, WHO ARE LIKE ME)		
MY SAMARIA (PEOPLE I KNOW WHO ARE DIFFERENT FROM ME)		
UTTERMOST PARTS OF THE WORLD (PEOPLE I DON'T KNOW, WHO ARE DIFFERENT FROM ME)		

WHAT IS MY SMALL GROUP DOING IN THIS AREA?	WHAT IS MY FAMILY DOING IN THIS AREA?	WHO ARE PARTNERS WHO CAN HELP?

DENOMINATIONAL RESOURCES
||||||||||||||||||||||||||||||||||||||||||||||

Excellent resources are available through many denominations. Be sure to research your denomination's website for additional assistance.

namb.net, imb.org, wmu.com, sbc.net

→ **Chaplaincy**
namb.net/chaplaincy-opportunities

→ **Community Missions in Your Town**
namb.net/loveloud

→ **Community Statistics Where You Live (Leadership Resource)**
namb.net/cmr

→ **Disaster Relief**
namb.net/dr

→ **Find My Local Association of Churches or State Convention**
sbc.net/stateconventionsearch

→ **How a Church Can Become Southern Baptist**
sbc.net

→ **Missions Trip Resources**
imb.org, namb.net, wmu.com

Missionary Opportunities (Vocational, Volunteer, Short-Term, Retiree, Student)

→ **In North America**
sendme.namb.net/involve-my-church
sendme.namb.net/missionary-opportunities

Mobilize My Church in Missions

→ **International**
imb.org

→ **North America**
sendme.namb.net

→ **Unreached People Groups and How Your Church Can Adopt One**
peoplegroups.org

→ **Your Job as Missions**
professionals.imb.org

→ **Work Your Job and Plant a Church**
sendme.namb.net

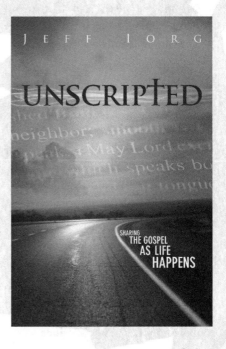

MISSIONS
Is a Lifestyle

FACES IN THE CROWD

Reaching Your International Neighbor for Christ

Donna S. Thomas
ISBN–13: 978-1-59669-205-3
$12.99

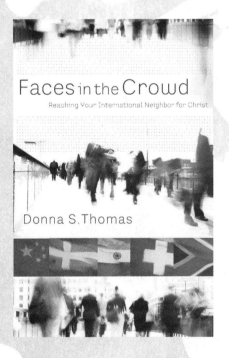

By sharing her simple and practical ideas, author Donna Thomas gives readers the confidence they need to become world-changing disciples. She advocates a missional lifestyle not a program. She covers the basics of international ministry: how to start a conversation, how to build a meaningful relationship, and how to work the Lord into ongoing conversations. With sensitivity, Thomas helps readers overcome their fears and then understand how to befriend and witness to people of another faith or cultural background.

||||||||||||||||||||||||||||||||||||||||||||||||||||||||||||||||||

New Hope® Publishers is a division of WMU®, an international organization that challenges Christian believers to understand and be radically involved in God's mission. For more information about WMU, go to wmu.com. More information about New Hope books may be found at NewHopePublishers.com New Hope books may be purchased at your local bookstore.

||||||||||||||||||||||||||||||||||||||||||||||||||||||||||||||||||

Please go to
NewHopePublishers.com
for more helpful information about
Across the Street and Around the World.

If you've been blessed by this book, we would like to hear your story.
The publisher and author welcome your comments and suggestions at: newhopereader@wmu.org.